WITH LOVE & LIGHT

A TRUE STORY ABOUT AN UNCOMMON GIFT

Jamie Butler

Published by Prime Concepts Group, Inc.
1807 S. Eisenhower, St.
Wichita, KS 67209-2810 USA
Toll-Free: 1-800-946-7804
Local: (316) 942-1111
www.primeconcepts.com

Printed in the United States of America

Butler, Jamie.
     With love and light : a true story about an uncommon gift / written by Jamie Butler.
     p. cm.
     LCCN 2008911338
     ISBN-13: 978-1-4392-2103-7
     ISBN-10: 1-4392-2103-0

     1. Butler, Jamie. 2. Women psychics--United States--Biography. 3. Spirits. 4. Spiritualism. 5. Future life.   I. Title.

BF1027.B88A3 2009   133.8'092
                               QBI09-200016

A Stranger In New York

"I'll have the curry soup to begin with, please." I say to the waiter. As I finish my order he picks up the last menu. I turn my attention back to my family and notice the sitar music in the background. Nice touch, I think. *There is something to be said about fine dining in New York City.*

Quite suddenly, I become aware of a stranger standing beside our table. Deeply immersed in conversation, his approach has eluded us all. Not wanting to be the one to admit to his presence, I keep my head hunched over my soup bowl. Peripherally, I notice waiters gliding past him and see his clothes are different from those of the other employees.

I glance across the table toward my parents and then at my friend Gentry, seated next to me, but no one is paying attention to this man. I'm doing my best to stay in the conversation and ignore his looming presence, but his imposition draws me out. *What does he need or want? It's obvious we are having dinner.*

I flash him an inquiring look. He is slim, neatly dressed, and appears to be in his late forties. I do not know him.

As I turn away he says, "You have got to go and talk to her. You are my last hope. I have tried talking to her but she won't listen to me. I know you can hear me. Do not pretend you can't. She is about to lose all her money. She is making a..."

My discomfort escalates as he begins sharing very personal details about an unknown woman's finances. I close my eyes and sigh, in an attempt to break away from his emotional outpouring.

"I am not your answer, please leave me alone. I'd like to be with my family in peace. Please...move on."

By this point everyone at my table is watching me.

"Who's there?" my stepmother, Jane, asks.

My words take a moment to surface. "You don't see him?" I propose half laughing but half serious, testing to be sure I'm the only one who does, especially since he is as real to me as the rest of the room.

An amused "no" echoes from the table.

Leaning in towards them I explain, "Okay...this man here says I have to talk to a woman in the restaurant about her finances because evidently her life savings are about to be taken."

"Which woman?" Jane requests, her eyes glimmering. She loves when these moments come along.

"It's..." As I scan the crowded restaurant a woman's aura lights up, as if by a spotlight. She is seated on the other side of the room in a dimly lit section. I gaze at the ceiling, wondering if there is a reason for her to be so illuminated, but there is no obvious light source. Pointing in her direction, I utter "that woman over there at the large table."

"Since this man is so persistent, maybe you should make an effort to approach her," Jane says. "If she gets up to go to the ladies' room you could follow her and give her the information."

We all look with anticipation at the woman, as if we expect her to follow Jane's unheard advice and actually go. At that moment the woman stands, pauses as if to excuse herself, and begins to move in the direction of the restrooms.

Turning to my parents I blurt in a low, pleading voice, "Oh, please, don't make me do this. New York City isn't like

Florida. You don't approach someone and say, 'Hey listen, I am psychic and this dead man who knows you is telling me about your personal life—mind if I share it with you?'"

Joel, my dad, stares right into my eyes, interrupting my excuses. "Jamie, there are no coincidences. You are not the one to decide who should receive a message and who should not. Just tell her what you were told. Don't you think it is more than chance that she is going to the restroom right now? Everything happens for a reason."

I look at Gentry for support but he remains quiet, almost disbelieving what is happening. I sense his withdrawal.

Taking a deep breath, I realize that my dad is right. Who am I to decide?

I feel like I'm about to perform a parlor trick. Shuffling my feet out from under the table, I force my body towards the women's room. My stomach tightens with each step.

What am I doing? This woman isn't asking for this. I can't lay this on her.

I turn the corner, and find myself face to face in attempt to reach the restroom door. She is stunning, tall and elegant—a model's figure. The fur collar of her fitted leather coat highlights her face. I'm dwarfed by her towering presence. *If only I could turn back.* She turns to go in first. As I reach for her arm, my hand brushes her elbow. She spins around with a quizzical look.

"Um, excuse me: I know you don't know me. But I…I have this ability where I…I am sorry to bother you, but I see people, I mean…spirit, and I am just trying to enjoy my meal with my family." *I feel so foolish.*

"I'm clairvoyant, or psychic…but I like using clairvoyant." I hurry on, "Anyways, a man appeared at my table and he is telling me your financial problems. He won't stop and like I mentioned, I'm trying to have a meal with my family. I am really sorry for interrupting your evening, but he makes it sound very urgent."

I look up at her, begging her patience. With one deep breath I begin to spill everything I had been told. "He is explaining how you took all your monies, savings, and especially the money you set aside for retirement and changed investors. The investor you recently fired is the old man with white hair who has worked with you for a long time and has a family connection to your father. Your father and he have done business together."

I check her face for signs of confirmation to what I am sharing, but she reveals nothing. Feeling miserable I plunge on, "The new investor is a young man with light brown hair, cut clean and short. He is a real sharp dresser and you pay attention to that because you like clothes. This young guy has high expectations and has told you a lot about how much money you will make. He's a real smooth talker. That's the problem, he is a smooth talker, and he is not telling you the truth. He is going to take you for a ride and swindle your money right out from under you. You've had a feeling in the past that something is not right but you can't put your finger on it. This is why you have not signed any contracts. It's not too late to get your money back. Is this clear to you? Do you understand what I am talking about?" I relax into my breath. *What is going through her mind? Her face shows surprise but no concern.*

"Yes," she responds eventually.

"Good. Please, do not lose your life savings. Go back to your original investor. Even though he is not as progressive, he keeps your money safe. Do not use the younger guy."

For the first time she looks away. I feel relieved, even confident that I did the right thing by informing her.

"Oh, and about the trip you are taking to Egypt this year," I add.

She swings back to me, "Yes?"

"Finish getting your ticket and go. It is going to be the time of your life and you will meet very important, influential people. Do you understand?"

She nods approvingly, appearing a bit shocked by this last comment.

"Okay, well, that is all he had to say," I tell her. "I guess I will go back and finish my meal before it gets cold."

Her jaw hangs loosely. Contemplating her words, she finally confirms to me, "Last month I transferred all my money to this new young investor, the one you just described, and I had an uneasy feeling about him, but the idea of making so much money must have clouded my judgment."

I smile encouragingly, hoping she will share more.

Her eyes become larger with surprise. "And how did you know about Egypt? I have plans to go later on in the year, but I didn't know if I would be able to make it. I already paid for half my ticket." Her voice fades out into thought, "So, *will* I be able to...hmmm."

Reaching out as if to hug me, she stops quickly and says, "I do understand. I really do. Thank you so much. Thank you."

Here's my break—I retrace my steps back to the table, feeling completely relieved that this unusual confrontation is over.

My parents eagerly wait to hear what happened. Gentry gives me the same uncertain smile I've grown to know. Getting used to this type of disruption in daily life can be difficult.

"Well?" Jane says brightly.

"I told her everything. She understood each detail and didn't ask about anything."

"Is that man still here?" Dad questions.

I turn to check just one more time. "No, he's gone."

"Don't you feel better about helping her?"

"Yes I do, Dad. Thank you for encouraging me." I gaze at my cold dinner, and start to eat.

Like a hooked fish, I'm released back into my ocean to

be myself. Set free to be caught again. Who will it be next time? What kind of message will be important? Why me? How can I ever explain this ability?

Contents

Introduction

With Love and Light was initially inspired through
a suggestion my father made several years ago.
Whenever I had an interaction with a client that
twisted my perspective on life, I would call him to
relay my experience and the impact the session had
on me. (I always respected the privacy of the people
involved and never used their names.) Because
this happened frequently, and my father found my
stories intriguing, he recommended I chronicle and
make them public.

These beautiful reunions, lessons, gifts, and information
became the basis of my writing. Many of the experiences I
shared with him are within the pages of this book.

The original premise for *With Love and Light* has been
refined through the writing process as the book took on a
life of its own. What I set out to create was a compilation
of sitter (the person who gets a reading) experiences written
by the individuals themselves. Interludes authored by sitters
have been included to open each part of the book, giving the
reader an exclusive point of view on psychic abilities from
different writers. I feel it is necessary to experience many
sides before creating a conclusion; this is my reasoning for
mixing in a multitude of different writers through out the
book. I am proud of the evolution and creative process, as

well as the brilliant influences of the chosen few involved, that has made *With Love and Light*.

I was born "open" with the ability to see and hear spirit, as most children are. Through socialization and assimilation into our world many children close their abilities off or choose to forget. I played with my visible friends (invisible to others) until age six when my parents conspired to "help" me leave them behind.

As I got older I didn't ponder why I no longer communicated with spirit. (I use the word spirit as a representation of any individual who is in spirit form. This is representative of both singular and plural usage.) Sometimes you don't know what you have until it's gone. In my case, I didn't know what I had until it came back. The evolution of my abilities is contained within Part I. My skills are not unique to me, but my life and the affect my abilities have on it is.

In Part II, I discuss some of my most unique experiences with the other side. My excursions in home (a place many refer to as heaven) have an unbelievable quality to them, but the lasting effect is as real to me as when I was there. I answer many questions in this section including: Where are spirit beings? Where is home? Is there a place called hell? What happens when a person commits suicide? What is an aura and how do I see and interpret one? And, I even translate advice direct from spirit who want to assist us along the journey of being human.

The final section, Part III, presents the initial concept for *With Love and Light*. There are twelve first hand accounts of persons who've had encounters with spirit through me. Many were reconnected with family and some received direct guidance from spirit guides. From family reunions to business advice, spirit assist where they can. I am pleased to offer you a balanced interaction by providing my viewpoint on these exchanges.

I received many submissions and I am thankful to all the people who were willing to share their story. Unless the individual discussed in this book has given permission for their story to published, their name has been changed and details from the reading are from my perspective. In the first hand accounts, names were changed if the specific author asked to remain anonymous. My family names are unchanged.

If there is one message that rings true over and over again from spirit, it is "what you believe in is your own truth." I only know my truth and I am not here to tell you what is true for you. I lay the full experience before you to draw your own conclusions. Psychic phenomenon can only be confirmed one person at a time as each individual has his or her validating experience.

If only for a moment, however brief, you suspend or broaden your belief in the afterworld, I will have achieved success in bringing this information to life.

I thank you for our meeting.

With Love and Light,
Jamie Butler

PART I:
Rediscovering My Gifts

Opening the Door

At eighteen it was time for me to begin my college education at the University of Florida, so I relocated to Gainesville. For the first year I roomed with my brother; after this, I moved in with friends Heath and Michelle, whom I adored. Heath was a drummer in a folksy rock band, "The Space Masons", that played regularly around town and we attended the same acting classes. Michelle was a friend from Lakeland—which is where I grew up—who had a carefree hippie outlook on life that could lighten everyone around her. Michelle and I got along like loving sisters and we shared many interests, the greatest being our intrigue with paranormal activities.

This mutual curiosity led us to sign up for a class called Psychic Awareness, offered as part of the community education program held at the local high school. I wasn't sure what to anticipate under this title, but I was willing to explore it. What I didn't understand was how someone was going to teach me "awareness" in only fourteen hours. Our class was to meet for two hours each Thursday evening for seven consecutive weeks. After completing this, Michelle and I hoped to walk away with the intuitive skills necessary to access the psychic realm.

We entered the classroom assigned to "Psychic Awareness" through a solid metal door painted turquoise. The classroom schedule taped to the wall fluttered as the wind gusted through the doorway and I quickly read that by day this room was used for Freshman English. Photographs of William Shakespeare stared at us from the surrounding walls as we each selected a coloured plastic chair from the circular arrangement in the center of the room. *Oh great! I can't even hide behind a table.* Lingering smells of old books and cleaners fumed up in the currents of the air conditioning, which hummed the perfect pitch to lull me into daydreaming. Under further scrutiny, as we waited for the other attendees to filter in, even poor old Shakespeare gave the impression he was suffering from the aromas.

Of the twenty-something people in attendance, Michelle and I were the youngest by nearly two decades. Our teacher Marguerite Romeis, an Italian woman in her mid 60s, started the class by having everyone stand and hold hands while she said a Catholic prayer interjected with spiritual words. "Not my style," I whispered to Michelle (who was Catholic herself). My initial discomfort subsided when Marguerite followed with a brief dialogue about how individual beliefs will directly influence spirituality and psychic gifts. She confessed that hers was founded on her Catholic background and was very respectful toward the diversity of her class.

Marguerite spoke with confidence when explaining how our bodies are made up of energy. She discussed how with every choice made we affect the well-being of our energy; therefore, we each are in direct control of our health. Seeing the disbelief on some of our faces, she provided a brief lineage of how this information was widely accepted in ancient cultures. *Where is she getting these details and why isn't it taught in science classes if it is so well accepted?*

I didn't want to ask questions and appear ignorant for not understanding, but I wanted to know more. I recognized during this first class Marguerite was only providing an overview and I would have to wait.

When she finally mentioned the ability to communicate to spirit, I understood her completely. The air conditioner clicked on and its sonorous hum resonated through my head, like bees in a summer garden. The calming effect of the buzz coaxed me down memory lane, distancing me from Marguerite's voice and into my past. My body relaxed and childhood memories of my six spirit playmates flooded my mind.

How quick and easy it was to fall back into those happy-go-lucky years before kindergarten. I had forgotten all about my friends. They were much taller and a lot older than me, around 35 years of age. Of the six, Bob was my favorite. I remember he worked as a businessman in Ohio before he died when his car accidentally slid off a cliff. Talking about their deaths didn't bother me; it was like an initiation they had to go through to be a part of our circle of friends. I knew all the facts about how each one of them died. For us it was as common as discussing what kind of game we were going to play that day.

Since Jason, my older brother by three and a half years, didn't believe in Bob, I always had to stick up for him. This caused a lot of fights between us for which Jason mostly got the blame for taunting his little sister. He truly enjoyed putting his finger in Bob's space to tease me or sitting in the seat I was saving for Bob. Sometimes he would even sit on him. Boy did that get me steamed!

My mom made great efforts to rationalize to me how there was not enough room for Bob in the back seat of the car. It was enough for her to contend with the two of us, Jason and me. We even had an imaginary line dividing the seat to prevent Jason and I from crossing into one another's space.

I can only assume my behavior appeared introverted and

unusual to my parents. Perhaps they thought I would grow out of the "imaginary friends" stage, but the older I got the more frequently they visited. No doubt all this antagonistic behavior was fuel for the fire that caused my mom to plot an ending to "this Bob guy."

After our weeklong vacation at our annual spot of Vogel State Park in the Georgia Mountains, we were getting ready for the trip back to Florida. My mother and I were standing in the parking lot between a green station wagon and our brown Pontiac Bonneville. My dad and brother were already in the car – waiting. I was six years old and for the first time my mother assured me that she had talked to "them." I was thoroughly excited because no one but me had *really* spoken with them. I had watched my family pretend to communicate with my friends in front of me, but I knew better.

This time was different; Mom was saying she actually chatted with them. She began by telling me how she had seen Bob and I having the most fun in the mountains. This little known fact won me over; she had talked to him all right because it was true. She said Bob told her he wanted to stay in Georgia and was afraid to tell me, which left her to be the bearer of bad news.

Bob lingered silently to the right of my mom as she continued. He offered no sign this was false information. Maybe he was waiting to see what I would do, but he didn't interrupt us. There had been no prior discussion between Bob and myself about him or the rest of my spirit pals staying but I had no reason to doubt my mother. She and I were very close and did tons of things together despite our differences of opinion about my invisible friends. I guess she was tired of finding me playing hide-and-go-seek or tag in the back yard with nobody, and listening to me chatter for hours, alone. At times I would save as many as six chairs everywhere we went. And even more bizarre, I would give her details about places I had never physically been.

And now she was telling me they had talked with her. I was convinced I had better say good-bye to them. After all, this is where they wanted to be, and to someone my age this reasoning sounded truly legitimate.

I strained to look up at Bob through the sun's rays as I leaned against the car and told them I had to go. *Goodbye, Bob.* Never taking my eyes off him, I scooted my back down the side of the car until I fell through the open doorway. I focused on my jelly shoes as I pulled the rest of my body into the car and pressed them against the back of the driver's seat. This helped me to be taller. The abrupt sound of Dad closing the door made me flinch. My final glimpse of Bob and the others was when I peered over the door's edge and watched them shrink in the distance as we drove away.

It was very upsetting to leave my best friend in a parking lot—homeless. I cried all the way back to Lakeland. About every 50 miles Mom would turn towards the back seat and remind me that Bob and his friends were staying in Vogal State Park while Dad quietly drove us home. I guess she thought I could conjure them up whenever I wanted. She didn't know they came and went as they pleased, or as they were needed. I believed they would always be with me. Never once did I imagine them not being there for me. For the first time in my life, I felt completely alone. I never saw Bob again.

Marguerite's voice seeped slowly into my consciousness until it drowned out my distant memories. "Not only can we receive messages from our spirit guides, we can receive messages from inanimate objects."

Our first lesson was to develop an understanding of psychometry. This is where a person holds an object and picks up images for the person to whom it belongs. Marguerite had everyone put a piece of jewelry in a paper bag to be circulated among the students. She demonstrated the different ways of holding an object in order to receive its energy or messages.

She cupped it in her hands, put it to her heart, placed it in front of her stomach and lastly, she held it to her head. I was reminded of the old Johnny Carson show when he was in character as the Great Carnac and would hold envelopes to his forehead giving the answer to the question contained within before opening it to reveal the query. I let out a giggle, which caused Marguerite to give me a sharp look. I bet she thought I was a cut up.

As the bag was passed to me I withdrew a ring. I checked to see if anyone was looking in my direction as I momentarily held the ring to my head to see if that would help my reception, but nothing happened. I found it most comfortable to hold it with my hands placed in my lap. *I am trying to communicate with a ring. I am trying to communicate with a ring. I am trying to communicate with a ring!* I felt stupid until I committed to the idea and cleared my mind, making it a blank sheet of paper.

Boom! Like firecrackers going off, my head filled with impressions. They sparkled in my mind's eye like an old reel-to-reel home movie; then the images shifted from small segments of video to photos. I didn't understand where they were coming from, but I immediately thought this was wild. I wrote off the incoming images because none of them made sense to me. These scenes were nothing I had lived or even dreamed about. After 45 seconds the images replayed. I accepted them at face value and figured I was done. I opened my eyes and watched the rest of the class concentrating for several minutes more. As I glanced around the room my eyes connected with Marguerite's. She gave me a look as if to ask whether I needed help, and I smiled a response of "I think I am done."

We concluded our first meeting by revealing our perceptions to the whole class. Several classmates disclosed bits of accurate information, while the rest seemed to have no luck. I gave details about a neighborhood white cat that persisted in making someone's yard his home away from home and how this was frustrating the owner of the house. *I wonder if this is making sense to anyone?* My classmates sat expressionless waiting for more.

I continued rambling, "In the same backyard there is a tree stump harboring residual energy about its healthy body being recently cut down in order to create space for white lattice work."

"You have my ring!" a woman yelled from across the circle. Before I could expose the ring, she began describing it to the class to prove it was hers and went on to explain how these were two situations she had been experiencing that very week.

As I returned the ring to its owner, I saw Marguerite keeping an eye on me from across the room. I guess I had passed some kind of entrance test. Later in the series of teachings, she invited a few of us, Michelle and I included, to attend private weekly teachings held at her home.

During the time I was taking the Psychic Awareness course, I began having shadows stand and run across my peripheral field of vision. These little tricks of the eye would catch me off guard. How unnerving it was to turn, expecting someone to be standing beside me, and only find empty space.

Spirit's interactions were becoming bolder and stronger. Electronic devices in the house became spirit's way of letting us know they were present. Sometimes after turning off the television, I'd step away and it would come back on again. The T.V. would also turn on and off like there was a power surge. Spirit would push the volume up and down when my roommates or I were watching a program. Heath would write it off as an electrical problem, but Michelle and I knew better. Before we took Marguerite's classes, we did not experience any of these unusual occurrences.

One night after returning home from school, I hooked my keys on the rack in our kitchen. I left the room to take a few minutes to settle in before I began studying at the table. When I went back into the kitchen my keys were swinging from side to side on the hook. I thought Heath was pulling a stunt on me. I checked for string, wire, magnets, or anything that could be attached to the keys. There was nothing except an extremely cold cloud around them, which I felt with my hands.

Mentally I tried to rationalize this mystery by convincing myself that someone must have touched them. I took a seat in the kitchen to wait for them to stop. A few minutes passed, and the momentum remained steady. I called out to Michelle and Heath to join me in witnessing this little phenomenon and to feel the temperature difference. I couldn't understand how they lost interest after five minutes when I was mesmerized. I stared, keeping time as the keys sustained swinging with great force until coming to a dead stop twenty minutes later.

Heath's viewpoint shifted a bit after this incident. He no longer blew off the stories Michelle and I relayed to him about our experiences. The key stunt provided us proof that spirit could move dense inanimate objects, and this catapulted my curiosity. I wanted more, and I asked spirit to show me. Looking back, I would now give myself a cautionary note like "Be careful what you ask for because you just may get it whether you understand its magnitude or not." I had no idea what would come my way from one simple request.

More tricks followed. The side door of my house would bolt itself without a key being in the lock. This was reserved for times when I retrieved the mail mid-afternoon. I would come back from the mailbox to find the door locked. After checking all the windows to gain entrance into the house, I would return to the door to find it unlocked. I was certain I had not locked the door in the first place, but I began second guessing myself. Granted, it took a key to turn this lock and my keys were inside on the hook in the kitchen. Talk about feeling crazy.

Before I went for the mail the next time, I looked between the frame and the door to observe the deadbolt unlocked, but when I returned the deadbolt was again in the locked position. Aha! Now I know I'm not crazy. This was not my imagination. Time after time, the bolt would unlock itself after I checked for another way into the house. I presume spirit believed this was funny. The one good thing about their prank was they never kept me outside for too long.

Their interfering didn't stop at physical manipulations. Voices talked for hours in my head, doling out advice, helping me with whatever project I was working on or directing me with how and what I should be doing spiritually to get on track. Chills ran up my spine from hearing my name called, knowing I was at home alone. I found myself frequently questioning people, "Did you hear that?" How could all of these messages be transmitted in front of groups of people and only be heard by me? It was like having on a decoder helmet that permitted me to pick up delicate signals from another dimension. I was confused as to why I was being singled out. If Michelle was also receiving this daily vocal interaction, I didn't hear about it.

There was no way for me to know that through attending Marguerite's classes I would reconnect to my childhood abilities. My current interest in the afterlife was reviving my ability to contact spirit. I would have liked to pick up where I left off with them, doing simple things like playing hide-and-go-seek. I remember my mom finding me in strange places when I played games with spirit. She would go into her closet to put away clean clothes, and there I would be tucked into the corner nook in the dark.

"What are you doing?" she'd ask.

"I'm playing with Bob and the gang," I would answer.

Much to my surprise, my mom recently told me she has only fond memories of Bob and the other friends. She said it was almost like having an invisible babysitter.

Back then using my skills seemed safe; my ability to communicate with spirit seemed to be solely for my entertainment. They played with me and protected me. My brother was another story.

One time he convinced me I too could fly like Mary Poppins—if I had an umbrella. This was one of Jason's harmless ways of taunting me; he never imagined I would test his knowledge out. I waited for an opportunity when nobody was around. Using the holly tree next to my bedroom window, I climbed onto the roof of our house and up to the peak, some fourteen feet into the air. I had one of those new retractable umbrellas that were advertised to fit nicely inside a briefcase. I didn't fathom that I might whiz to the ground like a lead weight. I expected to fly; therefore, I jumped.

The umbrella flipped backwards fast as I plummeted to the ground – but spirit softened the impact somehow and I landed on my feet without injuries. *How would I explain this broken umbrella to my parents?* Was my only thought. I didn't stop for a moment to contemplate the harm I probably escaped. I knew not to do it again, but inside I knew I could fly. I just didn't understand how—yet.

Spirit had greater aspirations for me than playing games, but they weren't too quick to share the details. There were too many demands, voices I did not recognize, and no peace in my life. There was constant chatter; my mind no longer seemed to belong exclusively to me. They were waking me in the middle of the night by gently rocking my shoulders or shaking the bed, and some would even sing at the top of their etheric lungs until I awoke. Often when I became lucid they would try to give me messages about my spiritual growth, but I disregarded them and fell back to sleep.

Sometimes when I opened my eyes, one or maybe two people stood at the foot of my bed. These weren't shadowy figures; they took the shape and density of people. It was difficult to distinguish if they were truly in physical form, and the anxiety that came with not knowing the difference was terrifying.

The day arrived when I reached my breaking point. Unable to endure the games any longer, I curled up on my bedroom floor with my back against the wall and huddled into some pillows. I stuck my fingers in my ears and began to cry. I pleaded for the voices to leave me. Rocking back and forth, I quietly repeated, "Go away, go away."

All I heard in return was, "We love you, you're okay, you're okay." I was confused when they consoled me and attempted to make me understand that everything was alright. I wanted the contact to stop! My spirit guides left me behind once before so why wouldn't they do it this time? This was too much to handle on my own, and I didn't have the strength for confrontation.

Crazy is the only word I can come up with to describe how I was feeling. Thinking that my Dad could help me through what seemed like an overwhelming crisis, I decided to call him. I remembered his silence in the car ride from Vogal State Park and assumed it meant quiet approval. I explained the voices I was hearing and the activity in the house. "Maybe I should go to the hospital to get medicated. Perhaps I am a classic case of multiple personalities like Sally Field when she portrayed Sybil."

My Dad chuckled. I didn't find it funny: I felt I was cracking up inside. But, he knew something I didn't. He convinced me to call my Nana, his mother. *Could she help me?* Although I am her only granddaughter, my Nana and I never exchanged deep personal experiences or confessions. But if she had answers for me, I was more than ready to listen.

I rang Nana and told her everything that had been happening. It was no revelation to her as she calmly told me, explaining how this type of ability runs in our family: from my great-grandmother, to herself, to her daughter (my Aunt

Carol). They all experience clairvoyance. It was only natural that I have it too, since it passed down through the women of our family.

Why didn't I know about this? As if she had read my mind, Nana confided, "It's not something we talk about." She was eager to share how she regretted not using her gift regularly, even though it was considered taboo in her generation. Nana thought if she had, she would have been able to rely on it more when she needed it. She went on to say, "You should study this gift and develop it in order to help others. You shouldn't keep it to yourself. The more you work with it, the more you can control it. It won't be scary after you learn how to use it. Carol had it real strong, but it was too much for her and she stopped it."

Our conversation enlightened me, but it didn't calm my nerves immediately. Just as I was looking for a way out or a medical resolution, I was being told this was an anomaly to embrace.

As a result I found the courage to go to Marguerite's private classes. She took me under her wing and nicknamed me "Little Devil," since I was the youngest person to ever attend her classes. (I'm also a challenge to teach because I tend to analyze everything.)

Marguerite taught me and others about meditation, intentions, dowsing, pendulums, reading auras, Reiki, using a psychomanteum, how to balance energies, the dynamics of the chakra systems, using Ouija boards, psychometry, psychokinesis, crystals, aromatherapy, out of body experiences and even Runes. But not once was there a lecture on how to manage myself as a medium.

When I surrendered to the path of using these abilities, I made a decision to use them for the highest good. To do so, it became necessary to make extreme changes in my lifestyle. I had to quickly adopt the habit of respecting my body when it was time to work. The concept was to keep a clean body so I would have fewer obstacles to work through to reach a higher level of communication with spirit. This is the same idea as putting a higher octane gas in your sports car. The old saying, "You are what you eat," was more accurate than I thought. I discovered my body would adjust its energy level to the item I was putting in it. Cigarettes, alcohol, white processed sugar products, and low nutritional food had to go. Ingesting these inhibited the flow of higher, healthy energy. I found twelve to twenty four hours after I consumed the inhibitors my energy level would balance out on its own. So I allowed myself to indulge on the weekends but the weekdays were for work, and I needed my body to support my ability.

I sifted through the techniques I learned with Marguerite to find a comfort level. Over the next few years, in a period of trial and error, I observed changes in my perceptions of people's auras, an energetic field which extends from the body, and how to interpret them. When I saw new colours or combinations of colour in someone's aura I would ask the person questions to develop understanding of what they could mean.

Within our class there were active students and those who preferred to stand on the sidelines. Because I was a willing participant, Marguerite would often call on me to demonstrate new techniques. Her favorite thing to do was place a chair in the center of the circle and say, "Jamie, get in the middle and give everyone a three minute- reading." At the time I was not too fond of doing this, but I'm sure this bolstered her confidence in my abilities.

Marguerite was one of the leading psychics at Gainesville's local Psychic Faire. Because of the infrequency of this type of gathering, it drew a crowd from across northern Florida. On the eve of a Psychic Faire about three years after I began her class, Marguerite phoned to tell me how sick she was and how she needed me to take her place and do readings. She didn't want to lose her reserved "hot spot" in the meeting hall; her table was set in front. Her station faced a wall of windows by the entrance, allowing everyone who came in to see her.

Somehow she convinced me to be her substitute. In her mind I was "ready." I knew I was a medium, I knew I could connect to spirit, but I also knew it wasn't something I was ready to do publicly. Feeling really thankful for all she had done to assist me in discovering my truth, I knew this was an opportunity to show my gratitude despite my discomfort with the idea.

I arrived early at the Women's Center with tablecloths, chalks, pen, and paper in hand. One of the ticket takers was nice enough to show me the way to Marguerite's table. As I was setting up, a few of the other psychics asked if I could help them. I quickly discovered they thought I was helping to organize the fair. I attempted to explain I was working as a reader too, but their patronizing nods felt like "sure you are." *Why was it so hard to believe I was clairvoyant, too? Was it because I looked too young?* I was only 21 and looked even younger. *You don't have to be over 40 with a crystal ball and a wart, you know.*

People were queuing outside the double doors, excited to be the first ones to enter. The other fourteen psychics had waiting lists; the only clients coming to my table were asking for Marguerite. I didn't understand why until a young college girl approached me.

"How can you be a psychic? You aren't old enough! You're like...my age! I really want to come see you...really, but I think I would be wasting my money."

Her comments caught me off-guard. *Is she kidding? Okay Jamie, how do you handle this?* Using my calm voice, I replied, "Okay...I will give you a reading and you can see for yourself. If, afterwards, you do not believe in my abilities, there is no charge."

My smile couldn't have been any bigger when half an hour later I accepted her contribution for my reading. To my surprise by lunchtime the longest line was at my table. People opted to stand and wait rather than leave their name on a list. Client after client received aura drawings and messages from beyond. Hours had gone by when suddenly I got the sensation someone was watching me. I peeked to my right and there stood Marguerite, a homemade lunch in hand, radiant with good health.

"Jamie, honey, I had to do it," she smiled furtively. "It's the only way I could prove to you that you are ready to be out in public." She confessed that she fibbed to coerce me into doing the Psychic Faire. *Now who was being the "Little Devil"?* Because of her integrity, I never suspected subterfuge and would fall right into Marguerite's sneaky schemes, which happened every now and then. I adore her for believing in me, for being firm with me, and for demanding I do better.

For eight years I studied with Marguerite, refining my skills. Without great teachers like her, many gifted people would not live up to their potential. She still calls with her sweet and nurturing voice, which I am always fond of hearing, to inquire about my work and well-being. She enjoys telling me how I have become the example for her new Thursday night students and loves sharing the story of how she coaxed me out of my shell. She says it's a great illustration for others to learn to believe in themselves.

I recognize how important it was for me to find a person with whom I could open up and share my truth. It is said that when the student is ready, the teacher will appear. Marguerite was the greatest supporter, mentor, and teacher I could hope for. She facilitated my growth in becoming comfortable with my abilities, no matter how out of the ordinary things seemed. I give her complete credit for my being able to share my abilities with others.

Awareness is a perpetual process and now I find myself in Marguerite's place. I started teaching classes in 1998 to help people reach inside to find their truth. It is important that I encourage people to change behavior and eliminate self-defeating vocabulary (like replacing "crazy" with more supportive terms such as "intuitive" or "gifted.") As more people nurture a belief in their sixth sense, the more spirit will be able to offer direct assistance.

Looking back, I now understand spirit seized the opportunity to reconnect with me. The channels I thought were shut down in my childhood had remained open. When I said goodbye to my spirit friends in Vogel Park, I closed off the communication and because they didn't seek me out again, I mentally locked the door to spirit. I often wonder where Bob and the others moved on to, but I accept that people, spirit included, have roles to play within our lives and may not always be ever-present. I do not blame my mom for being the catalyst of my disconnection; lessons come to us in many ways. This is the path I ultimately designed, and she was merely playing her part.

By taking Marguerite's classes I consciously chose to unlock the door, and spirit was more than ready to pick up where they left off. Since that chaotic reconnection, I have learned how to set boundaries that allow me to access my gifts when needed, and maintain a bit of normalcy in my life.

When my education in Gainesville wrapped up I was confronted with a new question: What do I do with this ability?

Chapter
– Two –

I Surrender

"Death is not the greatest loss in life.
The greatest loss is what dies within us while we
live."

–Norman Cousins

After graduating from the University of Florida, I decided to shift gears and focus on developing a career as a massage therapist. I enrolled in the Gainesville School of Massage, where I received degrees in massage and hydrotherapy. Mediumship had been a great way for me to work part-time and maintain myself for the eight years I lived in Gainesville, but I no longer wanted to focus on spirit communication. I didn't believe I could support myself solely by giving readings. Even though I had earned my parents' respect for my recovered abilities, for me, it was not a viable occupation.

Many facets of doing readings made me uncomfortable. Most clients came to my home expecting me to tell them completely confidential, personal, life- altering details. It was my responsibility to do this for them. The truth of the matter is; I am a hired secretary to connect the sitter to spirit. I transfer details or transpose messages from spirit. My only responsibility is to maintain my ability to communicate. Spirit has the task of confirming or revealing facts to the sitter. All I know is exactly what I am being told to pass along—nothing more.

Sometimes people needed more proof: it wasn't enough that spirit gave specific descriptions or facts. The sitter would push to know more, like "the one thing only spirit could know" that took place between them when they were living. The exhilarating and frustrating part was the majority of the sitters would get their answer but then proceed to tell me it was wrong because it was not the one they were thinking of. I wonder if the bulk of the messages spirit deliver are not received because the sitter has preconceived answers in their head. Having an open heart and open mind approach to readings definitely helps.

When the exchange is completed sometimes the sitter is in need of comfort, reassurance, or counseling, which becomes an awkward situation for me. Most of the time, I am entirely in the dark about what is going on between the sitter and spirit.

"If your spirit guides are not talking to me, I have nothing to offer," I explain. "I am not here to interject my opinion in to your life."

It's not my place to make sense of or assimilate this information for the sitter. It is uncomfortable to have people ask me questions after a reading like "What do you think they meant? Why do you suppose he said that? Was she saying I should do this?" I present myself very clearly as a transmitter not a counselor.

In addition to these pressures, I was confronted with developing a public image. When Marguerite received numerous inquires about my participation in the Psychic Faire, she would advertise in the news papers; "Jamie will be attending the Faire." On one hand it was exciting to be recognized, but on the other hand, I didn't identify with this new persona. I was uncomfortable being perceived as "the psychic." To me I was an average young woman: I took out the trash, biked to school, played with my Dalmatian, and accidentally over-cooked brownies until they were rock hard. But to others I was Jamie the Psychic.

Gainesville had given me a great deal of support and enlightenment, but it was time to move on. After several visits to my brother and his wife in Atlanta, I began to feel it would be a great place to live. I sensed I could make anything I desired happen there. With the support of my family, I relocated in August 1999, taking residence in a small apartment in Virginia Highlands. This hip neighborhood was just a few miles from downtown; shops, restaurants, and a few spas lined its main roadway. It had the feel of a village surrounded by a city.

My game plan was to keep quiet about my mediumship abilities and direct my energy into building a massage practice. I learned what some considered a precious gift was viewed as weird or suspect by others. Often, if a massage client became aware of my extrasensory ability, he or she would discontinue using my services. I learned it was better left unsaid. I did, however, keep this talent in my back pocket to use for friends and family, remembering Nana's nudging to refine the skill to help others.

I sent out professional resumes in an attempt to land a massage therapist position in an established practice, intentionally omitting my other qualifications. One of the first responses came from a woman named Lucille, a reflexologist. She phoned to let me know she did not have a position open but wondered if I could help her. Lucille told me that when she held my resume she knew I was gifted in other ways, and she had questions to ask. I was stunned. I started to explain that I was no longer doing readings, but before I could get the words out I found myself telling her information from her guides. So much for suppression. Lucille told me to hold on as she phoned her friend in California for a three-way conversation. She began ranting and raving about how good I was, "Go ahead and ask her a question on anything, she's the real deal. I found the real deal." I wanted to hang up the phone, but I promised to answer a few questions for her friend.

Well, I certainly underestimated the power of one voice. Before I knew it, Lucille had called me for several readings, after which I would receive a voice mail from another referral requesting an appointment. It wasn't long before I talked to her friends in California, New York, and a few other states.

Lucille recognized the importance of networking and since I was a newcomer, she shared pointers on where I could connect to build my business. She mentioned an upcoming convention that was advertised to be a huge affair. Only two months prior to the event, which took place in November, I secured a booth for the Whole Life Expo. Evidently space generally needed to be reserved a year in advance, but serendipity played a hand, and there was a cancellation on the day I telephoned.

Public opportunities were blooming everywhere around me. My new friends and clients took it upon themselves to set up interviews for me, and I agreed. I had not anticipated these types of engagements, but their reasoning made it sound like the logical next step.

One morning I was on a local television program on the NBC affiliate called Peachtree in the Morning discussing how I see and read auras. It was time well spent because the interviewer's enthusiasm for the topic made the discussion fun for me. It's nice when the facilitator leaves the platform open for positive interaction.

On another occasion I was a guest on a top morning radio show. This one was rough. Not only was I inexperienced with radio, but one of the hosts did not want me as a guest. He asked me to predict the weather. I'm a medium, not a meteorologist! He persisted asking me to tell him who would win the upcoming 2000 presidential election. "Even though the ballots are going to be read wrong, Bush will win," I said. Though the readings over the phone lines went well, the host cut me off saying, "I saved you because you were sinking." Although that was not the response I was getting from the callers, I felt like I had failed.

I also began presenting spiritual topics for small organizations and companies around Atlanta and realized I love being in front of people. Acting classes in college definitely prepared me for large audiences, but being in character and being myself are two completely different states. Speaking to groups about my personal encounters and abilities puts me in a more vulnerable position, and I feel an odd combination of fear and excitement. I never know in what direction I may be pulled. Some days I get an overwhelming feeling some person is about to grill me for the meaning of life. When the inquisition is accompanied by a "prove it to me" attitude I want to shrink up and run. On other days I am pumped with excitement from people's willingness to listen and their curiosity for the unknown.

My biggest fear in surrendering to this reality was the possibility I might lose myself, the "Just Jamie" part of me that is a living, breathing, and somewhat normal human being in the process. This feeling kept me pulling away from the public eye and distancing myself from media appearances. But destiny was pushing me to continue sharing my abilities.

Fate was orchestrating my course. My phone line was buzzing with callers from all across the United States. At the writing of this book I have reached people in over 40 states and in fifteen countries, including Belgium, Brazil, Canada, England, France, Germany, Portugal, and Spain.

I had to step back from my own perceptions of what it meant to be a medium, accept the truth of having these abilities, and begin to build a livelihood. At the same time my passion for giving readings was diminishing. The process was becoming too mechanized, and I didn't have the capacity to make a structured business out of a very personal ability. Outwardly I was succeeding at building a clientele and supporting myself, but inside I was failing miserably with my own spiritual understanding. After talking with spirit all day long, six days a week, the last thing I wanted to do was have another conversation with them, even if it benefited me personally. I began to feel numb towards the amazing interactions people were having during their readings. It was as if I was playing the board game LIFE but missing the real experience.

Something was missing. It was time to face my fears. I had distanced myself from Gainesville to prove that I could be on my own, free of training wheels. I needed an awakening, and my teacher was too far away to offer daily guidance. Of course my guides were witnessing all of this, but since I wouldn't actively engage them, they attempted to get through to me at night. I didn't respond to this tactic either – and so they sent Angela. This reading became my saving grace by bringing me a new perspective on how to surrender.

Quickly I gather the sheets from my massage table and put them on the floor. Although my previous client arrived late, I did not cut his time to keep on schedule. I choose to sit on my table and prop my feet up on a small wooden child's chair, which I use when working on a client's neck and shoulders during massage. (The table is much more comfortable than my rock hard antique couch, which was the only other piece of furniture to sit on.)

I shiver as a chill passes through me, much like the feeling I get when I am sleeping with my arm hanging off the side of the bed and sense someone is below who might grab it in the middle of the night. I decide to pull my legs up and cross them "Indian style" with my body completely on the massage table. The air conditioning struggles to work against the heat of the attic keeping my little one bedroom on the toasty side of comfortable on this humid August afternoon. My palms begin to sweat. Something feels different but I choose to ignore it.

I scan the clock as the phone rings. Why am I taking this phone call? Can I really help her? Doubt always seems to find me right before any reading. Then again spirit always shows up.

Angela's appointment was arranged last week. A friend of hers referred her to me. When I returned her call I set a date, a time, and confirmed the correct spelling of her name. This is all the information I have. To cover my lack of enthusiasm, I answer the phone in a cheery voice, "Hello? Angela?"

"Yes, it's me. Am I early?"

"No...You're right on time. I'm Jamie, nice to meet you. Are you ready to begin?"

"I guess."

"First let me ask you a question. Have you ever had a reading before?"

I always inquire in case I need to explain to her how this works. The more informed people are about this process of communication the more relaxed they become.

"No, I haven't."

After explaining as much as I could about me and how I work, a movement in the room catches my attention. Perched upon the small chair in front of me is a handsome man in his mid- 30s. The petite design of the chair causes his knees to bend close to his chest, giving him a nice place to rest his elbows.

Gazing directly at me he states, "I'm ready to talk. I am her father."

How can he be her father? The voice on the other end of the line sounds too young to have lost a father already.

He looks me in the eye for reinforcement. "Jamie, let's begin. I AM her father."

Confused, I turn my head to the side. This can't be right. How can this man be her dad? He grabs my attention by waving a white sign imprinted with bold black letters: F-A-T-H-E-R.

All right, I'll say it! I telepathically project.

I describe his appearance to Angela, as he repetitiously recites "father, father, father." I hesitate before telling her, "He claims to be your father. He is even holding up a sign with the word 'father' written boldly on it."

I sense her struggle to believe what is happening. She breaks through her silence to relate how my description matched the picture she is holding in her hands.

He begins to offer his life details to solidify her belief

that he is really communicating to her. "I passed away suddenly when you were a little girl. I had problems with my stomach. I want you to know that I have never left you. I have been with you all your life. You are not a victim."

Angela validates that her father died unexpectedly from a stomach ulcer when she was a little girl.

"I think we have the right person," I reply attempting to lighten an emotional situation, but I'm clearly not a part of this conversation.

Her father spends the next 40 minutes recounting Angela's life, spanning from what she wore at her first ballet recital to complete details of her high school graduation. He discusses her majoring in education and how wanting to transfer to another university could affect her and college credits.

She silently listens a thousand miles away to my recital. Angela confirms all he says, from advice on her lovesick roommate who wears glasses to the descriptions of the pictures hanging on her wall. Why is he giving her all these facts and not taking the time to talk with his daughter?

"You are not a victim, honey. Only if you want to be," he whispered and I translated. Evidently she had taken his death to be a personal punishment like she wasn't good enough to be reared by a father, like her friends were. He was encouraging her to remain strong by showing he had been there through every step of her life. He was here to illustrate that he, too (in addition to her mother) could recall her childhood.

"Jamie, I have only one memory of my father. Can he tell you what that is? If he is really talking with you he can tell you, can't he?" she asked with a demanding undertone. I knew this was her pass or fail question.

Here it comes. Her acceptance of this entire reading hinges upon the answer to one question.

Jerking the phone away from my ear I push it into my chest and plead, "God....if there is a Prime Creator, please let me get this right. Send me this message loud and clear. Please. Not for me, but for her." Every previous detail from this encounter would be wasted, all the love, all the amazing facts and apologies, if her father couldn't pass along this one memory.

A reassuring smile stretches across the father's face. He knows exactly what she means. Telepathically he feeds a scene into my head, as if I had a video screen, free from my imagination's control. I'm looking through the eyes of a tall person. From within a living room of a house, I cross through sliding glass doors into the backyard. The grass is green and uncut. My vision pulls back, and I see I have observed this scene through the father's eyes. A little girl runs to him. He grabs her under the arms and lifts her up and over his head, shaking her to make her laugh when her hair falls down around his face. The movie stops. Without emotion or judgment I share with her the images that overtake my conscious mind.

Dead silence.

Attempting to stifle a deep release Angela begins to speak, "Jamie...I only have one physical memory of...

of my father, and uh, that is when I was running to him in the back yard. He picks me up and holds me over his head and shakes me until I laugh. It was exactly as you saw it, only...I had a lollipop in my mouth."

She stumbles through a thank you, begins to cry, and the line goes silent.

After feeling the relief in this young woman's heart, I sit breathless. My legs and feet are stuck to the blue vinyl of my massage table. Spirit can really turn up the heat when they are working. God, I really believe you are there. I didn't understand at the time how badly I needed my gifts to prove to me that spirit, Prime Creator, and the afterlife are real, reachable, and tangible.

I was overwhelmed with the realization that what I possessed was far greater than who I am, and larger than I could comprehend, and humbled. I was startled into admiration of the potential growth my connections could bring and confronted with the reality of knowing this was to be my future, and my level of responsibility would escalate. This ability held the power to transform, heal, and help people, as well as spirit, on their journeys. Deep within myself, I resolved to make this ability my life's work. I knew it could come with great sacrifice, but for the first time I truly felt ready to surrender.

This was the shift I needed, a reminder to maintain a higher level of sensitivity and positive regard with each individual. My experience with Angela filled me with a profound love, a sense of peace, a fascination for things to come, and yes...it humbled me greatly.

I immediately called my dad and sobbed, "I love you,

I love you. I love you, I love you..." until his answering machine beeped. Setting down the phone, I cried harder than I have in years.

Chapter

— THREE —

Relating to Family

*"It is not nearly so important how well a
message is received as how well it is sent."*

—Neale Donald Walsch

Reconnecting to my clairvoyance created new dynamics
between my family and me. It didn't take long before we were
all acclimated to my abilities and how the communication to
the beyond could serve us. Not everyone reached out for the
experience of communicating with the spirit realm, which
was fine with me. My mother's family generally doesn't ask
for my assistance while my father's side (where the ability
derives) embraces it at any given moment.

Dad inquires about certain family members, checking on
health and illnesses for others. This questioning generally
takes place around the dinner table after a meal. With a tooth
pick in hand he will announce, "For dessert we have Jamie
giving everyone a reading."

One time his grandfather came for a visit. Granddad
Freeman reminded Dad about "Hiroshima." He asked,
"How do you like your cottage at "Hiroshima?" At first I
didn't understand what Granddad Freeman was saying. I
understood the 'hero' part of the word and interpreted what I
thought I followed-'mosa'- hero-mosa. Dad got a kick out of
this and explained that when he was a kid, his parents would

send him and Aunt Carol to Granddad Freeman's home in
Rye, New Hampshire for vacation. Granddad Freeman had
a knack for collecting items, displaying them prominently in
the side yard along with a flagpole stuck in a mound of dirt.
His reasoning for calling his home sweet home 'Hiroshima'
was because he felt it looked like a bomb was dropped on it.
Dad says it is fascinating to hear details of our family from
long before my time.

Jane extended her assurance when she asked me to do a
group reading for an upcoming family reunion to be held at
their home. This was my first group reading.

I was very nervous about conducting a group reading.
How was I to know what information was too personal for
me to reveal in front of a group? Spirit made it easy for me
by saying, "Tell them to raise their hand if the messages
are too personal and you will talk privately with them
afterwards." I followed their advice and the reading went
smoothly. Everyone enjoyed the experience and no toes
were stepped on.

Jane set up the living room with candles and dimmed
the lights. Ambiance is her middle name. She set out chairs
arranged in a circle so everyone could see each other. I could
describe the entire evening but find it useful to give you
another view point on the evening. Jane gave her notes on
how the group reading went.

"When I hosted my family's annual reunion, summer
of 2001, my step kids joined in to everyone's delight.
My cousins were excited to finally meet Jamie and a
group of about 10 of us asked her to give a group
reading. This was the first time Jamie met my cousins
since they all live in different areas of the country."

"Jamie started the session by telling us the room was
crowded with people and each of us had a group around

us. Of course everyone wanted to know who was there and when Jamie started to tell us, a very demanding spirit interrupted her. When she started to describe this lady, everyone in the room, except for Jamie, knew whom she was talking about. Jamie described perfectly my Aunt Pauline who had passed on about a year and a half earlier. Aunt Pauline was the mother of two of my cousins in the room. I had the feeling they all thought I had given Jamie this inside information by the looks I kept getting. I'm sure they thought Aunt Pauline's death way too recent to be the butt of a parlor joke.

Aunt Pauline understood her girls' skepticism and shared some information only they knew. Apparently she was embarrassed about her weakened condition in the last months of her life as she was confined to a wheelchair. She hated the wheelchair and made her girls swear they would not tell a sole that she could not get around by herself. When she relayed this information to Jamie, and described the floor plan of her home and difficulties she had maneuvering the chair into the bathroom, both of my cousins burst into tears. They realized their mother was there in the room with us and they went on to receive some advice their mother wanted to share with them. Lastly, Jamie went around the room to each one of my cousins giving them messages from this unseen dimension."

My favorite memory from the family reunion session was the old man dancing. He said he was one of the seven uncles and identified which one by giving his age and describing how he died. Then he broke into some sort of dance. Imagine a late sixty year old man, pot belly and skinny legs, throwing his arms in the air and wiggling his body around. He was not telling me what he was doing; he just danced. I found his behavior so funny that I laughed and imitated him for the whole family to see. I wanted them to understand why I was cracking up. Everyone enjoyed my show, and they knew what he was doing. What I interpreted as dancing was actually him doing his play call positions. He was a referee! After their laughter subsided they clued me in on the specifics.

My dad also challenges me to give readings on the spot. He throws out names of people and I convey messages about them that relate to Dad. The beauty of answering his questions is Dad always put the information in his back pocket and decides what to do on his own anyways. So I don't mind telling him everything I know about the people he names, he makes his own opinion. He especially loves to invite his unsuspecting friends over and have me cold read them. He will search for any kind of coloured pencils, crayons, or variety of ink pens for me to draw auras, bring me a stack of blank computer paper, and then he becomes the conductor of ceremonies. "Now, Jamie will entertain you. Just watch, you don't have to do anything. She'll tell you everything."

Joel even took it so far as driving me over to his friend's house as a surprise and have me read their auras. He would not tell me anything about his friends not even their name until we arrived. He got his friend to get a box of crayons and told them to sit back because you won't believe what you are about to hear. I began with the owner of the house breaking down the colours in his aura and discussing how his personality conflicts with his wife's and how to compensate this. Needless to say the tension in the room was thick and no one was talking except for the occasional ohhh, ahhh.

My parent's friends made them promise and swear several times that they had never told me anything about them. Many times they glared at my parents as if a practical joke was being pulled on them.

"I have not told her anything!" Jane says. "She's reading your strengths and weaknesses, likes and dislikes in such detail, even your own spouse would have had a hard time doing such a good job."

Jane, my Dad and I were all amused with the accuracy of the information that came through. Joel topped the evening off with this statement which made me blush, "You should see her when she is talking to your spirits."

Joel and Jane love this type of "entertainment." I really don't mind because it shows their confidence in my abilities. They are willing to put friendships on the line and risk embarrassment if their daughter is wrong.

There have been many moments where my abilities reveal truths that are kept from me, whether out of protection or forgetfulness I'm not sure. For example, my family and I recently went to bury my great Uncle Dana in Rye, New Hampshire. We met with my dad's cousins, whom I had faint memory of because my Nana's side of the family didn't have reunions when I got older. The last time I saw them I was around five years old, they didn't know much about me so the only work topic I discussed was massage therapy. (I call massage my Clark Kent cover when I choose not to discuss my other skills. This could be a copout, but on occasion it is the simpler route to take.)

The second night in Portsmouth my dad decided the family would have a reading, or maybe a channeling session. He invited all the cousins, their children, and his parents, Nana and Papa to his hotel room. I arrived a half hour early to get focused and get acclimated to the idea of channeling for family I barely know. It was a bit uncomfortable; what if they did not understand? Spirit reassured me everything would be okay.

My parents were propped up on the bed and I pulled out the only chair in the room and claimed it as mine for the night. I began to focus and call their spirit guides in when I looked up to see my step grandfather, Jim, Jane's father. He told me how happy he was now that Millie was with him. Millie, Jim's wife, as far as I knew she was still alive. I was shocked to see her standing next to him, but he certainly was thrilled to have her home. When I told my parents what I saw, Jane whipped around and grabbed dad's arm.

"I thought you were going to call Jamie and tell her," she quickly blurted.

"No, you said you were making all the phone calls." Dad responded.

"Yes, but you were talking to Jason and I thought that meant you would call Jamie next." Jane turns to me, "Jamie, Millie died the day before you left a week and a half ago. We already had her funeral."

Millie jumped in before I could react to what just happened and offered personal messages to Jane about all the work she did to help Millie and her family.

Grandpa Jim explained they would be on vacation for a while and would not be able to come around. They said their goodbyes and left.

And this is how I found out my step grandmother passed away.

My mother and stepfather, Joyce and Dale (whom I call Papa), have not asked me to use my abilities. They understand I can do something that is uncommon and maybe even mystical to them. Even though we don't sit down and talk about the details of my clairvoyance or how I work, they acknowledge me in their own way. Papa peering over his glasses casts me a reassuring look of 'all is well' and tells me, "You're special in some way and we know you are always kept safe." My mom confesses, "Out of all our children, we never worry about you. Maybe this is the reason why." She smiles and hugs me. Despite the fact they don't inquire about my gifts I know they understand me as much as someone who knows and receives my work.

My family and I have tested my skills in many ways. My brother has been the most creative in employing my talents. In college Jason convinced me to go with him to bars in order to tell him who had an interest in him. For the record Jason is not a player, he is shy. Because of this he had a hard time meeting new people. So we set up a system: I sat at one end of the bar with my glass of water while Jason was at the other end.

Each time Jason found someone he looked at me and I would either signal "yes" by raising my glass in the air or "no" by waving my hand in front of my throat. My response depended on the appearance of the woman's energy field. If a woman was attracted to Jason her energy would glow outwards towards him, as if reaching out for a hug. If the interest was not mutual the woman would pull in her energy, much like putting up an invisible force field or barrier. There was success to the system and it was a way of mixing fun into being clairvoyant. After helping Jason, I would turn to the bartender or the drinkers next to me and test my skills even further by giving them readings nonchalantly to see their reactions. It was good practice, believe it or not. There were people in the bar who would normally never come to see a psychic medium but were intoxicated enough to not be bothered by it. I kept the messages short and simple – a bar is not a place for intense lessons.

My family has adjusted quite well to my being public with my abilities. Now we are able to discuss psychic traits openly in public, it is no longer the hush -hush topic kept to a whisper. The first time my Aunt Carol, Nana and I had an opportunity to talk about our family traits in public was during a walking tour of St. Augustine.

The sign read "Walking Ghost Tour of old downtown

historic St. Augustine, the oldest city of the United States, as seen on Discovery Channel." I lined up 35 of our closest friends and family members on the old cobble stone streets. It was 10 PM – the last tour of the night, which I figured would enhance the spookiness of it. It was my ingenious idea to gather after my wedding rehearsal for a little fun and offer everyone a chance to see a ghost or feel the chills from the stories of old.

Everyone was huddled closely around a graveyard (the final stop of the tour), when Aunt Carol and I stepped away to see for ourselves what or who could be lurking within the gates. Nana was a few feet away from us. The tour guide was doing her best to deliver a captivating recount of the story about a beautiful young woman who died on her wedding day. It is said she roams the graveyard at night looking for her lost lover. Most of our group was into private conversations and disappointed because no ghost had vaporized to scare them. I was kind of hoping not to see her because I thought it might be a bad omen considering I was getting married the next day, but there she was in her flowing white gown about 45 feet away from me, floating across the cemetery.

Aunt Carol came up behind me and asked if I saw her. Simultaneously we described the lady in white: where she was, how she moved across the grave plots and down the path. We looked at each other and laughed. I don't know if it was out of relief that someone else saw the same thing, or because we unsuspectingly shared a secret viewing. Nana overheard everything and confided her knowing that we would see something. In some strange way I felt like we were in an ancient witches' gathering.

The following day, in addition to my best friend dedicating his love to me by becoming my husband, I received an enormous gift. Surprisingly it was not in a neatly wrapped box or placed upon the gift table.

With champagne glass in one hand and a microphone

in the other my Dad announced, "This toast is going to be a long one so I'll wait while everyone gets another drink."

Minutes later Joel began describing, in great detail, the most embarrassing moments of my life. He shared with family and friends how I tried to steal my car back from him after he grounded me and left for a weekend vacation. (He had resourcefully removed some wires from the engine so it could not start and parked it on the steeply sloped hill outside their house. Pushing that car back up the hill was an act of God!) Our guests were laughing and crying at the same time from my father's impassioned recount. This crescendo was followed with a recital of *Sunset*, a poem I wrote in sixth grade that won the state competition.

My Dad has a talent for immersing people in his stories. Every five minutes he paused to encourage the guests to refresh their drinks. *How long is he going to talk? I can only take so much embarrassment, Dad.*

I anticipated a more traditional toast about relationships, honesty, commitment, and love, not a momentous recanting of my past actions. Then the unimaginable came. While my three-tiered cake was beginning to tilt in the humid Florida air, he closed with an apology for he and my mother's dissolution of my contact with the other side when I was a child.

I didn't realize how much I needed an apology from my parents.

My heart sank deep; I felt it beating in my toes. All the sound ran out of my ears, I looked at my Dad with disbelief. (The photo in my wedding album is a definite keeper; I was so shocked my eye brows vanished in my hair line.)

I do not know why my Dad chose this public moment for confession, but for me it was a quiet victory amongst my extended family and friends.

I admire him for his willingness to stand at my wedding take the blame for making me "three dimensional, rational, and logical."

"We molded you into this perfect world of ours. Sorry… Jamie, with my years of background in science, fact-seeking and statistical data analysis I can't prove to others this talent of yours." Dad's words came with sincere reinforcement, "I feel it like the wind against my face, don't see it- don't need to. I know I'm comfortable with the faith. Your readings are a gift, a revelation; some might say an intuitive trust."

My Dad continued to mend all the perceptions I had of myself when I was growing up. Standing next to my cake, a model of the leaning tower of Pisa, he told all 120 wedding guests that his daughter was not crazy, that her imagination was vivid but her communication to her "imaginary friends" was real. There was laughter and words of joy from my close friends and my teacher Marguerite.

I looked at my mom, Joyce, who was sitting down behind Dad; she was grinning from ear to ear. I don't know if she knew beforehand that Dad was going to say this but I knew she too was one hundred percent behind every word said.

Twenty-three years after the Vogel State Park confrontation, I was forgiven for being weird. My Dad put his arm around me and told me he was proud of me; proud that I did not let the closest of idols persuade me into changing what I knew to be real. I survived my parents' desire for normalcy.

PART II:
Inside a Clairvoyant's World

Brian's Search for Pascal

By Brian Dyson Vice Chairman, COO [retired] of
The Coca-Cola Company, author of *Pepper in the
Blood*

I was in my late teens when I began thinking about
my span of life—born in 1935—and that I might
reasonably last through the Millennium. This
prompted thoughts about passing on...what happens
then...and finally, what is the purpose of life?
Perhaps this was because I was reared on the Pampas
of Argentina where the sheer vastness of space lent
emphasis to the finity of my allotted time. I did not
consider myself presumptuous; I believed that others
also struggled with these thoughts and, similarly, did
not share them.

A few years later, whilst rifling through a moldy
reference book, I found a small typewritten card and
my thoughts leapt to a higher plane. My mother had
printed a passage from Pascal's "Pensees", circa 1656.

*"When I consider the brief span of my life, swallowed up in
the eternity before and after, the small space which I fill and
even see, engulfed in the infinite immensity of spaces which I
know not, and which know not me, I am afraid and wonder to*

see myself here rather than there; for there is no reason why I should be here rather than there, now rather than then."

The words resonated deeply provoking me to enroll in a Philosophy class and wrestle with dense texts that questioned our very being. Surely pursuing Pascal and the other great thinkers was a loftier cause…and I shelved my studies in Business Administration.

Soon I was disillusioned. The scholars I met with weren't going anywhere. Too consumed by their methodical doubts, they only came alive when discussing Descartes by wine and candlelight, with a few deep-eyed and intense women for when the candles burned down. Reluctantly I tucked the Pascal quote into my wallet and returned to the less glamorous pursuit of a career in business. At least it offered a roof over my head and might even lead to travel, plus it fed my burgeoning curiosity about the whole world out there.

After a depressing start, fortune smiled and my business career took me to many places and made me a citizen of the world. But even as I sat at rich tables and mingled with the powerful, I was ever faithful to my original passion. The Pascal quote, which had passed from wallet to wallet in my service, was ever with me. I knew the quote by heart and was always ready to argue his case with quiet vehemence. Where was Pascal now? Surely his life had not been snuffed out like some wasted candle when he died at 39? What careless deity cast such a brilliant intellect aside; is that all there is to life? The words still ring in my mind, "… the small space that I fill…". A few wretched decades and then you're gone…Forever?

"That's right," said a cycling friend of mine. "Once it's over, don't expect any after-life. None of that 'through the wind tunnel toward the light' crap that Khubler-Ross talked about. When it's over, it's over. Dust to dust. Believe it." His pitying tone only fueled my resolve and I rebelled at the seeming pointlessness of life.

Is there no purpose? Is my father just ashes? Is there a Supreme Being who now views us as a primitive experiment—to be discarded like used toys? Poor Pascal. Poor me. Poor us.

I did research on Pascal that rewarded me with a further defiant quote. "Who has put me here? By whose order and direction have this place and time been allotted to me?"

As I ascended the corporate ladder I had less time to ponder these verities and Pascal remained mostly confined to my wallet. And when the Millennium came and went, I dutifully sighed with relief that the phones still rang, planes flew and ATMs continued to dispense instant gratifications. Like sheep, we all came out of our mental bivouacs thankful life went on, without a serious thought as to where or for what purpose.

It was in this late afternoon of my life, when I began to lapse into complacency, that Pascal came back to me as if the urgency of his quest had burned a hole in my back pocket. The same poignant questions, the same earnest entreaties to ponder our wretchedly small space, came flooding back – only this time with tantalizing, potential answers.

"Spirit is just as much a part of life as we are," my new friend Jamie says, "only different."

As I struggle with this impossible truth she smiles kindly, "You could see them too...and talk to them. Anybody can."

I know she is being charitable, but the gates are now open and I'm off on the hunt. My conundrums come blazing back, back, all the way back to my early restlessness on the Pampas in Argentina. *So there might be a purpose after all?* The question beckons. *Can I be enticed? Should I explore?* I find myself peeking into the mirror and hoping to glimpse a Spirit Guide – yes, one of my very own.

I let a few weeks pass and now my curiosity becomes more intense, my questions more focused.

"It will come to you," she says. But her soft assurance seems oceans away, as a reminder of how far I must travel.

How does she read auras, or contact spirits in a reading? Does she flick a mental switch or just shift into some spiritual Drive? "They just show up," she says. The placid certainty with which she speaks leaves me no doubt. I search her face for clues. She is warm and present—and yet—not here. I turn away from the steadfast gaze.

Can this young woman be a reincarnation? She never claims to have any past remembrances. "You're not supposed to," she says simply. "Not in this life." Did Pascal recycle? Might I? I must find out more.

More time passes. My mind burns with the same old intensity and I am compelled to go through this new looking glass. I now feel a distant hope that down some long and winding path, I may at least come close to finding Pascal.

I seem to have finally come full circle. It has been a long, lonely journey but I'm here at last. I must ask Jamie for a reading. I will prepare myself for when the moment is right.

Chapter
— FOUR —

Where is Spirit?

"All I have seen teaches me to trust the Creator for all I have not seen."

—Ralph Waldo Emerson (1803-1882)
The Best of Ralph Waldo Emerson

When I was a little girl I would have said, "Spirit live on Earth because they are standing in front of me." My adult perspective allows me to answer this differently; even though they appeared to be on this plane, spirit are actually in another dimension and have a higher vibration of matter, which is not exactly "living on Earth."

Recalling my eighth grade physical science class, I understand the basic principal of matter: dense objects have slow moving particles and lighter objects have faster moving particles. The faster the molecular movement, the less dense the object becomes. It reminds me of the trompe d'œil of a ceiling fan. The faster the blades spin the more transparent they become. Relate this principle to spirit beings and human beings…you guessed it; the denser objects are living humans and the lighter objects are spirit. Nevertheless, you want to have a higher level of vibration; I do not suggest spinning as fast as a ceiling fan.

In order to communicate with spirit I increase my vibration through meditation or relaxation, while spirit simultaneously lower theirs. Thus, we are able to connect on a mutual plane. I learned how to do this through my studies with Marguerite. It sounds more difficult than it truly is and when I began learning the how-to parts of this skill it all seemed a bit out of reach. The frequent misconception I see people having is believing that meditation, relaxation even hypnosis for this matter, takes the person "deeper." I understand it is common to see relaxation as going deeper like floating to the bottom of the ocean. But if that were the case then the view point from the bottom of the ocean is pretty short sighted. Look at relaxation as when the body lets go of Earthly daily thoughts, stress, and aches and pains, what can be considered weight, and see the body going up into the sky; like a helium balloon whose weight was untied from it's string. The view point from here is endless and in this space, one creates a heightened state of awareness. Perspective changes everything.

A friend of mine inquires, "If you can do this so easily and that's all there is to it, than can't EVERYONE do it?" My answer to this is "Yes, but generally people prefer to look outside for answers than communicate directly; a person would have to be willing to take responsibility for what may take place. Generally people have high expectations and may not be willing to go through the learning and discipline process to reach this level. We each choose different paths before we incarnate and mine included having this ability and helping others. Not everyone signed up to be a medium." If you want to learn more about the scientific explanations of energy and vibrational measurement check out Dean Radin's, *The Conscious Universe: The Scientific Truth of Psychic Phenomena.*

Through years of studying spirituality, I have discovered there are many levels in which spirit beings are located. There are three levels I most frequently discuss with people who are curious about death or transition, each is known by various names. The titles I use are ones taught to me by spirit guides. The In-Between place is where souls who chose to linger on Earth reside after they pass over. The Healing Space is for souls needing energetic repair and/or individual purification due to a traumatic life or passing. And lastly, there is the place most commonly referred to as Heaven, which I affectionately call "Home." Home is a central place where spirit gather between lives and journeys.

In Between Place: Where Lost Souls Reside

Though most spirit beings go to Home after leaving their body, my guides consistently tell me everyone has a choice. This gift of choice is known as "freewill." You have the option of going Home, or choosing to avoid it and remain on Earth in spirit form. The souls that choose to bypass Home (for whatever reason) become Lost Souls residing between the two locations. In Between suggests the soul is in limbo, caught between living on Earth and Home. I compare In Between place to what some religions call "Hell." My guides have taught me there is not a place called Hell for the reason that God would not abandon, remove freewill or damn anyone to a place far from his or her reach.

The term God for me is representative of masculine and feminine. For me God is a non-denominational androgynous universal energy. I will refer to this being in the masculine as "he" from here on out but this is only to save me from having to reference "he or she."

Being In Between does not have to be an eternal existence. There is a safety net for Lost Souls. If a Lost Soul has the slightest thought of any being who is in Home, they will receive intercession, an opportunity to cross over to the realm of Home. This thought will manifest an exit represented by what suits that soul the best (a doorway, a tunnel, etc.). Ultimately the choice belongs to the Lost Soul. Even a soul in the In Between place has freewill.

The perceived environment of In Between is directly influenced by belief. Spirit see what they choose and more often than not this transfers from the life they were living. The irony of these situations is paranormal activity can be a two way street. The Lost Soul inversely sees what we experience as paranormal activity. Our movements interfere with their reality of In Between. This causes confusion for both parties and a mediator literally becomes necessary to clear this debacle. This is where someone like myself can facilitate the situation.

In my experiences "ghosts" do not truly mean to harm. An encounter is equally confusing to the ghost as it is to the humans involved. Imagine trying to communicate while being invisible to most eyes, silent to most ears, and the easiest way to get attention is through tangible objects. I might be provoked to move items around too. It is their misunderstanding of their state of being that causes interference in our world. They may not recognize they are dead, let alone, a Lost Soul. The movie The Others wonderfully depicts this scenario.

One Lost Soul I assisted was an elderly man who passed before his wife. He lived with her for 50 years in the same house and remained there after his death, waiting for her to pass over. His determination to continue living with her was keeping him on the earth plane. He assumed if he left their home his hope of finding her would dissolve.

For nearly 20 years after his wife's death he remained in their home waiting, all the while becoming more baffled when the new residents took over his bedroom where he kept watch over his wife each night. Little did he know he had missed her transition. When his beautiful wife died of old age she went straight into the light and Home, skipping over the In Between place where he expected her to meet him.

The current owners were entertained by the paranormal activity and knew the house's history because their realtor explained the previous owners had built it. They had a vague idea of what was happening, but needed assistance finding a possible resolution. The residents were distant friends of a mutual connection. After hearing their story I knew if the old man ventured into the light he would discover the love of his life waiting for him. My role was to convince him of this possibility.

I found the man in his bedroom standing in the farthest corner from the door looking around the room. His brown pants matched his short sleeve plaid button up shirt and his hair was almost nonexistent. After a brief introduction, he told me his dilemma. His voice sounded sad, but I heard strength behind it.

I suggested he might go somewhere else to find his wife.

"I told her I would wait for her here, and I am," emphasizing the "I am."

We argued for some time because he was being stubborn and single-minded about the possibility of there being a better meeting place. I again mentioned going somewhere else, but this time I used the light as the destination.

"Let me tell you, I have never broken a promise," he said.

"You know, if you do not find her there, you can come back here and wait for her. If she shows up while you are gone, I will tell her to stay here until you return for her. How does that sound?" I replied.

His face had a curled up expression full of new hope. "But how can I trust you? What if I can't get back?"

My choice was not to focus on his negative questions but encourage him to think of the light. After doing so a bright white glow appeared behind him. It was a kind of portal or doorway. This haven of light was not enough to convince him to find her elsewhere. Again after a long discussion of where he could reunite with his wife, he chose to peek inside the illuminated area. Backing away he turned to tell me his wife was there with outstretched arms beckoning him, but he was hesitant to step into the doorway. His inflexibility made me laugh. The image of his emotionless face turning towards me and breaking into a smile is etched in my memory. I bet he hadn't smiled in over 20 years. He apologized to me for being argumentative as he slowly walked into the light for what was sure to be a loving reunion.

When a soul resides in the space of In Between, they maintain their personality, but more often than not they encompass a lower range of energy. They will exhibit lower level emotions like anger, jealousy, guilt and pity. Some souls will even be revengeful if they are disgruntled with how they passed or have what they feel is unfinished business. This is generally caused by confusion or denial of what has taken place and most often occurs due to an abrupt death, such as a suicide or any accident, leaving an individual wondering whether they have truly passed.

Here is an example my guides gave me of how personality traits persist in Lost Souls through addiction. If the Lost Soul was addicted to alcohol when living, then he can also be addicted to it in spirit form. How this works is soul will find himself a human that shares the same addiction and like a feeder fish on a shark, the spirit attaches him to that living person and feeds off their energy. This is done out of comfort for the Lost Soul but to the living person this is known as having an attached spirit being or entity, which can create an upset in the human's energy field.

Great conflict can arise when the human tries to quit drinking because the alcoholic Lost Soul can attempt to persuade the human to continue by manipulating their energy; very much like the fictitious little Angel and Devil who sit on your shoulder giving you directions on which choices to make.

Before you think you might have an attached spirit

preventing you from achieving a goal, I must inform you the human involved has to be willing to allow this Lost Soul to be present in their energy. Just like the shark can turn and eat his feeder fish friend, so can the human refuse to have any spirit attachment by protecting himself through intention. Spirit attachment can also have a positive influence; for example a spirit who has crossed over into Home can assist a human by being a personal cheerleader, advisor, or guardian angel.

Hauntings and Poltergeists

On another occasion I was called to help a family who are friends of my stepmother. At the time, I didn't know much about dark energies and had no idea what I would encounter in this home. It became a great learning experience, but going into it I was clueless and went with my gut instinct on how to handle what I discovered.

On arrival at the two-story house in South Lakeland, I was told there was a spirit haunting three of the rooms; the main bedroom in the upstairs loft, the baby's room at the base of the stairs and the living room directly across from the baby's room. Regardless of the family being at home or away, the spirit inhabiting the home was rearranging furniture in the master bedroom and living room. Chairs were being pushed down the stairs and the couch was frequently moved away from the wall into the center of the living room.

The children were afraid to be in certain parts of the house because a creepy feeling overcame them. Since moving into the house, the family developed mild illnesses. Everyone that is, except the baby. Their attitudes had become grumpier and they frequently squabbled. The spirit's aggressiveness and anger was fermenting in the house like rotten tomatoes in a jar, causing an imbalance in the home's energy.

I entered the house through the kitchen after surrounding myself with golden white light of protection and calling on my spirit guides for assistance. I got an unnerving feeling they wanted me to do this on my own. Following closely behind Jane, we passed through the doorway into the kitchen. Immediately I felt sick to my stomach and my head ached. Even Jane admitted she felt the heaviness in the house. I told Anne, the owner, I would walk through the house taking notes of what I found and then explain my findings before making an effort to do anything. I didn't have a game plan, but the sheet of white paper I held was a reminder to remain as open and clear as possible.

Walking up the stairs, I received a strong mental suggestion that I was going to be pushed down the steps if I did not leave. Immediately I thought of *The Exorcist*. This definitely was not the time to spook myself more than I already was. I recalled the part where the priest advised his helper to repeat the Lord's Prayer. *Okay.* This sounded like a good idea, but not knowing the Lord's Prayer completely, I substituted an incantation of *I am above you in love and light. I am surrounded by white love and light.* I repeated this in the same cadence as Dorothy in The Wizard of Oz when she says, "There's no place like home."

I had to refrain from showing fear, both inside and out. Fear feeds its source, and I definitely did not want to empower whatever was in this house. As I moved through the bedroom, waves of heat overcame me followed by gushes of cold wind. It was as if there were air conditioning vents every ten feet in the walls oozing out cold air. As far as I could see and hear the spirit was not present in this room, but there was an overwhelming sensation of whatever was present was willing to do harm. I cautiously descended the staircase, guiding myself hand over hand on the single banister to keep stable as I headed towards the living room.

Crossing the large open space of the living room I announced to the spirit, "If you are here I would like to see you. My name is Jamie. Anne asked me to come over and talk with you. I am not going to hurt you and you will not hurt me." I threw in the last clause hoping "it" would understand I did not want to fight. Still…there was no reply.

One room remained to be explored. I slowly walked over to the doorway of the baby's room and peeked in. There it was! A huge swirling mass of energy, dark blue and mossy gray in colour, in the far back left of the room. It loomed in front of the closet door. Seeing this gave me the willies and I nearly tripped over my feet backpedaling into the kitchen to tell Anne what I saw.

She shouted in amazement, "That is the exact place where I get the creeps the most. That is why the baby's clean clothes are on the floor – I can not go in the closet!"

"I'm going in there to try to talk to it."

Summoning all my courage I entered the baby's room. The hairs on the back of my neck and arms stood on end. Nausea ran through me as if I had food poisoning. *If only I had a proton pack like the ones used in Ghost Busters. I wouldn't be so damn scared.* I took a seat on the daybed and demanded to the unknown entity, "Whoever is here, step forward so I can see you. I need to talk with you because you have…" Before I could finish my sentence, a very tall man, nearly six and a half feet high, wearing armor was standing about eight feet in front of me. Defensiveness glared from his face. His presence caused my stomach to turn deeper with a warming sensation. An imaginary belt tightened around my chest. *I'm protected in white light and I cannot be harmed.* (White light has a higher level of vibration than what he was able to create himself, being a Lost Soul, so I had the upper hand in that department.)

I told the vengeful spirit calmly, "We need you to leave this house. It is not yours." *Probably not a good thing to say to an aggressive man in armor.* Rephrasing the demand, "I meant, why are you living here in this house?"

"This is my land, my house, and my child. I will not leave," he spoke with a rasping authority and conviction. *Thees ees my land*...clearly a Spanish accent. The temperature in the room started to rise.

"Why do you feel as if this is your land and your house?" I emphasized how he felt since I did not know the history of the property.

By the look on his face I saw he was getting irritated from my questioning.

"I founded this place. My men and I camped here and provided food for the soldiers. We farmed all this land that you see," his tone angry and militant like one accustomed to giving orders.

"What happened?" I inquired while the nauseous feeling continued bubbling in my stomach. I was mindful to keep my face relaxed showing him my passivity.

"Why are you here? You do not belong here. Leave while you can." He retorted.

"Are you trying to threaten me?" I charged back at him. Then more calmly I added, "Because I am here for peace. I am not making you do anything. I only want to show you that there is a better place for —"

"I will make you leave," he authoritatively interjected. "I will make you sick. I can do what I want – this land is under my control."

He spoke with such force I believed knives would fly out of his mouth next. I don't know what held me to the bed, but I stayed. I knew he could not harm me because I protected myself with light and my empowering belief in it kept me safe. Although I was uncomfortable talking to him, I knew it was the time to change tactics and ask him personal questions, remaining cautious not to antagonize him.

"What happened to you? Did you have a family?" I could instantly see I struck a soft spot. I relaxed my posture, but stayed alert and ready to defend myself.

"I had a family, one son and a wife until they were

murdered," he revealed, giving me a threatening look. "My whole camp was murdered when we were ransacked by the Indians. I was left to die. My head was fixed to the ground and my eyes made to stay open so I had to watch my family die first."

"I am sorry that someone treated you that way." I was as compassionate as possible with him. "Are you still with your family?"

"NO! They were taken from me!" his arms went up into the air to match his loud voice.

"Didn't you go through a bright white light when you died?"

"No. I take care of the farmland. I have to provide for the soldiers. This is my duty. I have to keep watch to protect us from the Indians."

I knew I had to guide him to think about his family. This was the only topic that changed his energy to a soft blue colour, which meant he was willing to talk calmly.

"Do you want to see your family again?"

"I see my son; he lives here in this house," he said pointing at the ground. "He came back to look for me."

I started to understand. He was confusing Anne's son for his own. That was why everyone was getting sick except the baby.

In an attempt to clarify the facts for him, "I know Anne's son lives here, but I do not know of any other little boy that lives here. Can you show me?"

The grimace on his face was a sure sign he was irritated I didn't understand him the first time. "I live with him here in this room. I protect him from the people that live here. They are Indians."

He thinks Anne's family is Indian? "Listen, Your son is not here."

"Do not tell me I am wrong."

"Do you want to see your wife?"

"Yes," he said without hesitation.

Now I have leverage. He wants something. Here is my opportunity to give him directions and hope the love for his wife will give him the curiosity to follow. "All you have to do is imagine a doorway and she will be behind it." He must have indulged my suggestion because a doorway of light appeared behind him. "I have seen your wife and son." He stared at me like I was setting him up. "It's true. They are behind you, inside the beautiful lighted doorway. Why don't you try turning around and seeing them too?"

"NO!" he yelled forcefully causing me to jump back on the bed and draw in my feet. My back was against the wall; I could not get further away from him without leaving the room. I had no idea what this man was capable of and I didn't want to know. *How do I turn this to my advantage?*

"I understand that you are in control, but if I was as strong as you I would not be afraid of a door. This place is no longer what you want it to be. Anne lives here with her family—not yours. We are living in the year 1997. Turn around and face your family that needs you!"

As soon as he turned around and saw them standing in the doorway, I heard a loud cry of pain like all his demons were drawn out of him. Before my eyes he transformed into the man he was before his dreadful death. The vortex in the room swelled up and vanished.

A cool breeze cut through the heat and I felt like a tornado whirled through me. I fought the dizziness and wiped the sweat from my face; I could not move from the bed. *What just happened? Did I do the right thing? Is he gone?*

My guides appeared. "Jamie, he passed through the light and is with his family. He has been released from the In Between and is on to his own healing path."

How convenient for you to be here now, after I did all the work. "Where were you? This is not in my job description.

I like to talk to spirit beings, but I do not want to tell them what to do. I am not a recruiter for Home."

A soft thank you was all I heard in return.

I told Anne and Jane about the man and drew a picture of his armor. Anne bugged out and told me she had been dreaming about a man wearing armor like I had drawn. She sketched it on paper she kept at her bedside. This puzzled her and she did research, finding details about Spaniards who traveled from St. Augustine to Tampa through the land her home was built upon. Anne and her husband had extracted artifacts from their property as well, but were unsure of their origin until now.

The lid was opened and the jar cleaned out. I am very happy to know that after this experience Anne's family feels comfortable being in any room of their house. It was an experience of a lifetime helping Anne's family, but it is definitely something I choose not to do again if possible.

I have great respect for the people who choose to perform exorcisms and spirit releasement work. They need to be great mediators; I like to view them as the lawyers of the spirituality. One needs to know how to convince the other to become open. This is the state of being which is needed to progress. The "lawyer" does not need to persuade the spirit to believe in a certain path, only to help promote freewill to the spirit. They also need to be able to discern between spirit possession and negative energy disruption. Most of the home hauntings I have heard about through colleagues are actually caused by collected negative energy. As an example; if there was a murder at the Jones' home and they move out so the Carter's can move in. Then the Carter's have an abusive father who uses foul language and pushes around his family. The father's negative energy combines with the negative of the murder. This collection of energy can actually disrupt the natural flow and cause the inhabitants to feel there is another presence in the house when in reality there is not. This is the top reasons to bless, clean, sage, feng shui, or in extreme cases exorcise your home. An energetically clean home is a healthy home.

Healing Space

When a human being has a traumatic life or passing the soul is intercepted from its path to Home at the time of death and sent to the Healing Space. Keep in mind the power of freewill can override this destination and place the soul in his chosen environment, such as the In Between.

A soul is sent to the Healing Space depending on his or her ability to heal properly. If a soul cannot heal on their own from their past life's influences and repair their energy tears, holes, depletions, etc., they will be sent to the Healing Space. Here is where one's soul can be freed from past memories long enough to heal. The soul in this surrounding can now be able to view the positive inflections of all the negative actions from their old life without having attachments. In many ways it is like receiving the gift of seeing your life in third person with the knowledge of interpretation. After healing is complete the soul is moved on to Home. This process is also known as being cocooned.

I have heard this place referred to as the Healing Center too. The reason I call it "space" is because this safe haven has a black background with no walls, no boundaries. There are swirls of vibrant colours: greens, blues, violets, and white. This is how I believe super novas appear in space.

The only time I have experienced the Healing Space is during a past life regression with Dr. Brian Weiss, MD. I was a student at his one-week intensive seminar on Past-Life Regression at the Omega Institute in Rhinebeck, New York. I was volunteered by a third party to be the subject of a demonstration for the class. Dr. Weiss used a rapid induction technique to assist me in reaching a deep level of relaxation and heightened awareness: hypnosis. To understand more about Dr. Weiss's technique and background look for his books, *Many Lives, Many Masters, Through Time into Healing, and Only Love is Real.*

Dr. Weiss first asked me to think of an issue I was working through in my life. I chose "searching for love." He guided me back into my childhood, then back into the times before my birth that related to my issue.

Before I could analyze what was happening I found myself in another lifetime. I felt like I was in an oversized body with rough facial hair and I was digging potatoes out from around small rocks on the hillside where I lived. The sensations were comparable to being in a dream where every action I took felt real, yet I was actually sitting in a chair. Dr. Weiss walked me through the terrain until I reached my thatched home of two rooms. During this lifetime I was a farmer in Ireland.

I met my wife. Her looks were aged by her work in the sun, but this did not matter to me. I loved her more than anyone I had ever met across any lifetime. I was confronted with the difficult decision between staying with my wife and going to the war. Her words to me were, "I waited seven years for you to return from the last war and if you leave, I would gladly wait ten more, but please — this time stay for me. Stay for love."

Upon hearing those words I knew that life was more than work, war, and surviving. I knew that life was solely about loving who you are and who you desire to become. I could not bear to leave her again. I took the risk and told the town I could no longer fight. I suffered a great amount of ridicule, so much that I spent the rest of my life on my farm while my wife attended to the needs in town, though I had never been happier.

Dr. Weiss's voice guided me to look into my wife's eyes. He said I would know if her eyes belong to anyone in my current life. When I focused on her eyes I saw the eyes of my best friend Rui. This was a bolt from the blue to know that we had a love so strong. I made a conscious choice not to tell Rui this had happened. Dr. Weiss then directed me to the latter part of that life when I was to pass over. I was bedridden for months with sores all over my body. I could feel their tightness, the burn, and the ooze of moist fluids on my clothes. The pain was so intense it was almost non-existent. My wife had already died and my two sons were caring for me. I could not hear their voices for my ears were boiled with growths. My fever felt as if it could melt my body. I finally let go of life but instead of seeing light, I saw complete blackness.

This was a surprising comfort to me. I was weightless, cool and free to move however I wanted. Then swirls of light came into the space. They appeared to be entities of their own. Green, violet and sky blue light brushed against me. I began to forget all about my suffering. I was given a message in my head that my energetic body was too damaged and I was sent here to finish my healing. I would stay here until I was complete. I understood it was my responsibility to heal on my own and I would know when the process was finished.

I heard Dr. Weiss's voice coming through again asking questions about where I was. He had other patients travel here before me and the comfort in his voice assured me I was in the right place. Dr. Weiss told me I was being healed from the inside outward before I could continue. He let me stay here for a moment before he asked me to return to present time. I remember telling him "no, not yet." I was intrigued there were other places to go to when you pass away. I am positive there are more destinations I have not yet been shown. He allowed me to sit for a while to recap my life lessons from the Irish farmer lifetime; the major learning was about choosing love.

Later in the same month I took a working trip to

Portugal with Rui. He was to help me by acting as translator in the readings. After several long days of delivering messages from spirit, we retreated to the Azores Islands. The atmosphere certainly lived up to its legend of being Atlantis. It was here I finally felt comfortable enough to confess to Rui how much I loved him and that I was ready to be more than friends. He must have understood how serious I was because his response was, "Are you sure? I've waited for you for four years and I'd wait ten more." I was shocked to hear him repeat the very words of my past life wife. Before I could answer him I began telling him about my regression experience with Dr. Weiss. Finally with every part of my being I knew I was choosing love. One year later to date, we married.

Home

In the space of Home (Heaven), there are several levels spirit inhabit depending on the knowledge retained through multiple lifetimes and on lessons completed. Spirit beings interchange on these levels based upon the work they are doing. I have been fortunate to have had two opportunities to visit this extraordinary place.

Granddaddy Jones passed away when I was fourteen. At the time I was not in touch with my abilities and the loss of him hurt deeply. I did everything with him. Every chance I got I worked with him in the woodshop building things, or I would catch him on his break, sit with him under the orange trees and eat too many oranges, as usual. Five years passed before we met up again, first through my dreams, until I was emotionally comfortable seeing a vision of him again, and then "in person."

Granddaddy loves to enter into my meditations and talk with me, especially when I am in an inquisitive mood. One day I asked him questions about death: what happens, how does it feel, where do people go?

Granddaddy took my hand and led me down a tunnel of white light. I remember laughing in disbelief, "You have to be kidding me. I thought the tunnel existed because someone made it up and everyone believed it."

"There are several different ways to come Home. This happens to be the most common. Whatever you believe death to be like is how you will experience it."

I did not respond to him after that. I had to think about what it really meant. I had heard and read of people who believed they must meet their demons before continuing into to Home. I silently thanked myself for not believing in that path.

We floated to the end of the tunnel and sat on a bench located inside the end. I saw a group of people gathered about thirty feet away waving and smiling. The colours were brilliant and clear, unlike any spectrum I have seen here in our physical world.

"Jamie." He put his hand on my knee. "This is not your time to go so you cannot stay here for long. There is no need to fear death anymore…it's no longer a mystery."

He was acting sneaky, which led me to think he was not allowed to bring me here, but I was grateful he did. The smell of saw dust lingered on him from the workshop where he taught me how to use woodworking tools. We held hands as I remembered how much I miss him in my daily life.

The moment went by too quickly. We stood to leave, but I did not want to go back. Granddaddy went the return length of the tunnel with me.

"Goodbye Grandbaby. I love you the mostest." He whispered as he leaned in to give me a kiss. We always tried to outdo each other for the amount of love we had for one another.

Granddaddy was right. Since that moment I have not feared death, the experience brought me a certainty and knowing of what is to come, which brings me a sense of comfort.

A Guided Tour

My second journey Home was even more intense and happened when I was going into a deep trance to channel information for a client. Channeling is where I relax enough to step out of my body and allow another spirit to come in and use it to communicate with people on this side. Channeling is a process that merits respect and should not be taken lightly. Most of the time when I channel it feels like I'm falling asleep. I don't remember the information or the spirit beings that come into my body unless I am allowed to stay and observe by the spirit who is channeling through me.

This time while I was going into a deep relaxation a female spirit whom I had not met before offered that I stay aware and watch — as long as I did not interfere, meaning I could not talk, which is hard for me because I am always asking questions.

I felt like Charlie in *Willy Wonka and the Chocolate Factory* when he won the golden ticket. *I have been granted admission?* A huge smile stretched across my face, partly because this spirit looked like Xena from *Xena the Warrior Princess*, but mostly because of my amazement that they would allow me to see what until this point had been beyond my boundaries.

Xena told me I was ready and since I had been requesting to learn more, today would be my opportunity. Every year on or after my birthday my abilities grow stronger and deeper. This particular year I had been asking to be able to see other dimensions and receive knowledge about the afterlife. I felt like she handed me the key to a city.

I found myself stepping away from my body and following her about two feet up and away from the floor. As I stood behind my physical form I noticed how brown my blonde hair is turning with age. Another spirit was getting permission from Granddaddy, my gatekeeper, to enter into my body. When I channel it feels like I drop out of existence and because of this I want someone to help me monitor how my time is used. I chose Granddaddy not only because I trust him, but also because I have a history with him. He decides who is allowed to enter into my body and who is not. This incoming spirit entered my body through the back of my neck when Xena motioned me to look upward.

I could still see the Native American patterned rug beneath me as the walls diminished, shrinking smaller and smaller until out of view. A mist of white light crept softly around my feet. What my eyes were seeing was something I could only conjure in dreams yet the sensation of being in it far outweighed the whimsical state of dreams.

Glancing up toward my left I watched as three enormously tall angels appeared. They stood at least nine feet tall, each gleaming a distinct colour; the first was blue, the middle one violet and the last one pink. All three had wings positioned back and up as if they were going to fly over my head. I imagine wings to be made of soft white feathers, but theirs were slow swirling masses of thick energy. Not wanting to look like a novice, I contained my excitement and questions, remaining as quiet as a mouse. And of course, not talking was the deal I made in the beginning. This was not my first time seeing angels, but it certainly felt like it. As surreal as my journey felt thus far, there was more to come and I needed to stay alert.

To my surprise Home is only two feet off above the Earth. My analytical mind kicked in with my brain in overdrive. I thought Home would have been much further away, above the clouds, amidst the stars. Now it all made sense: when I was a child seeing all the spirit walking around on my level, I was actually witnessing them in the space of Home, not Earth. I was mixing my worlds or dimensions.

To the right of the angels was a woman dressed in a white robe trimmed in blue, clothing similar to a nun's habit. She motioned for me to move toward her. I knew the image of this woman but could this be real? I approached her in amazement. I was being introduced to Mother Mary. I felt paralyzed. Even though I knew little about her from a religious context, I understood why she came for me. She represents to me a spiritual woman who exudes unconditional love without judgment for all of humanity. These are two personal goals I share with her. The fragrance of roses swept across my face as I stood squarely in front of Mother Mary. My chest filled with flutters and I found myself softly weeping as a gentle force of energy passed through me. I reminded myself again, *this is not a dream.*

Mother Mary blessed me and spoke directly of my path on Earth. She told me about my gift of teaching, how to always speak my truth and also to be grateful when my truth changes. Those moments would mean I was growing. She filled in the missing pieces for me about my career and healing abilities. Mother Mary did not use excess words. I did not know how to thank her properly so I chose to kneel down, bow my head and be grateful. When I moved, my body felt as if I could float away, as swiftly as the wind glides through leaves on a tree.

Redirecting me, Xena touched my shoulder and pointed me in a direction where I could go off on my own. At her invitation I got up and started moving. A building in the distance caught my eye (and my thoughts) and suddenly I swept past the greenest of grass, immaculate gardens with footpaths, flowing waterfalls and people of all ages as I instantaneously found myself at its entrance. This was at the top of an enormous set of smooth marble-like stairs. The doors were made of glass and strangely they were without hinges. *How do they work without falling off?* I pondered.

As I absorbed the panoramic view I was very surprised to discover I was within a city. Everyone here appeared healthy and strong. I noted the median age of the people to be around 30, or maybe they were mimicking my age?

Quickly I entered the building, encountering level after level of neatly organized scrolls. A woman in white greeted me. Speaking telepathically she explained to me how every scroll was arranged in alphabetical order and by merely thinking of the name I needed, my body would instantaneously go to it.

"What if a person's name has changed? How will I find them?"

"Any name old, new or spiritual will lead you to the correct chronicle of that person's lives. Allow your body to show you. Only think of the person's face and your destination will appear." I could tell by her smile, she really loves introducing new concepts to others.

I was distracted by trying to remember these details and truly forgot about my body. My hand tingled as I touched my chest, but it did not stop at what I know to be my physical perimeter. *Wow...I feel solid, alive, and vibrant; better than I have ever felt.* Dropping the line of inquisition within myself, I went on to check out the library.

I thought my name, *Jamie Butler*, and glided all the way up to the 6th level, straight to my scroll. I removed it from a small compartment and unraveled the scroll to take a peek. My spiritual name and Earth name were imprinted in the top right hand corner; along with my birth date and location were astrological symbols mapping the location of the stars and planets at the time of my birth. Below this information were details of my life goal, all the lessons I have chosen to learn and the happiness I incorporated into this lifetime.

Various words and lines were blacked out like a top secret FBI government file. At first I wanted to complain, but I understood this necessity. Spirit beings are there to guide, assist, and help. They are not permitted to interfere with our lessons or hand over information that needs to be learned independently while we are living. Often I wish I could have gotten the undisclosed details, but I know I will benefit greater from the life lesson. I looked further, seeing line after line cataloging my lives and a list of people with whom I have had interactions. The scroll went on and on. It was incredible to see all of these particulars documented. Suddenly I became aware of my time limitation; I returned the scroll and left.

Outside on the steps were groupings of people. I stopped to inquire for the time. My human mind was still governing my movements. I needed to know how long I had been here so I could guesstimate how much time I had left. Did I ever get a head full of information! In the future, when I understand it more I will attempt to explain what happened. For now it will suffice to say that time is a manmade element and Home is a timeless place.

Off in the distance I saw Xena. I was sure she was coming to take me back to my body. My desire to be physical had diminished through my exploration in this plane and I wanted to figure out how to bypass the return. Thinking it through thoroughly, I evaluated my family, my love for my brother, and how he would understand why I left. I knew I could even visit him from here. My boyfriend, my dog, it all ran through my mind and not once did I believe I would miss them. I never felt more whole, free, light, and completely loved. I knew this was unconditional love. I knew I was home and I was determined not to return to Earth.

Astral travel is fast. Xena and I arrived at my body instantaneously. Again I could see my dirty blonde hair as I poised my spirit body to refuse reentrance to the physical. I stretched my limbs outward like a cat trying to avoid being shoved into a kitty travel box. *There is no way she can force me back in there!* A look of apology shined in her eyes as she gave me one swift encouraging push. Reeling in the dense reality of the third dimension, I found myself back in my body gasping for air.

My heart rate was sky high. How unfortunate for my client. I bluntly looked at her in disgust and said, "I do not want to be here. I am not meant to be alive. I know where my Home is!" I paused, looking for a spark of understanding from her and then burst into tears. I cried and cried in anguish until my chest hurt. This had never happened before and afterwards I felt silly for reacting this way with my client. I am grateful she was a caring person who asked me questions and offered consolation.

It was awfully painful to return with memory of where I am from. I cursed at the spirit beings who forced me to come back into this place. My body felt heavy, clumsy and awkward. I was overwhelmed as I looked around at my office observing my collection of books, art and assorted items. I had too much stuff! At that moment I wanted sell off everything I owned. *I can become a nomad, own one pair of shoes and trade for all my life's expenses.* These feelings persisted for nearly thirty minutes before I relaxed into my old self.

I apologized to the sitter as I attempted to explain my journey. Every word exiting my mouth made the experience sound less than what it was for me. I would have sacrificed my ability to speak to keep the feeling of being in Home. That is how much the trip affected me.

I have not been invited back to Home since this occasion. Although Xena said I was ready, I feel like I wasn't emotionally prepared to see, feel, or experience Home because I miss it too much. I am in awe of the event. It took me a while to come to terms with the value of what I had been permitted to do.

At a minimum this experience gave me the proof I needed to know there is a place where spirit gather regardless of gender, race, religion, or spiritual persuasion. The memories bring me great comfort and have facilitated my truth about life after death. All lessons come when they are needed.

Chapter
— FIVE —

The Reading Experience

"Man is made by his belief. As he believes, so he is."

—The Bhagavad Gita (500? BCE)

Communicating with spirit

There are many ways people can communicate with spirit beings. These encompass abilities like *clairvoyant*: the ability to see beyond, *clairsentient*: the ability to feel beyond, and clairaudient: the ability to hear beyond average capabilities. All humans have the potential to communicate with their guides. When it comes to psychic ability and intuition, everyone has the basic energetic makeup and channels in which to connect to the higher dimensions. The key is: as long as you believe communication is possible you will be able to achieve it.

We each have the means which can be refined and polished to allow us to shine in whatever field we choose. For example, humans have the physical structure to be able to swim. Swimming can be for exercise, play, or survival. When an infant is placed in water, the first thing she will do is hold her breath; this is an innate instinct for survival in the unfamiliar environment. As we grow older we have the choice to refine this ability and learn how to swim. We can take lessons to teach us different styles of strokes. Soon we can decide if our abilities are strong enough to continue. Some people may choose not to swim and only to stand on the steps or wade into the water knee-deep. Even though we can all strive to be Olympic swimmers most will stay within our comfort zone.

Communication with spirit is very similar to learning to swim. We each are born with innate intuition. Through development and socialization we expand or diminish our connection. Some of us will remain open from birth while others may never tap into these channels.

One of the easiest moments for spirit to communicate is the time before falling asleep or waking up, before "reality" sets in. This is when a person is in the alpha state. Alpha state is one of four brainwave frequency patterns produced by our brains naturally. Beta state is when we are alert, active, and using all of our senses. Alpha is a more relaxed state and occurs mostly when we are dreaming, which is known as REM (Rapid Eye Movement) sleep. Theta occurs in a deeper state of mind and has been found in people when they are hypnotized. Delta state is the deepest of all, though not much is known about it.

In alpha state, your vibration is raised due to total relaxation and the mind generally lacks conscious focus. Spirit beings can lower their vibration level to match your heightened one — making communication possible.

Meditation makes this same process possible for you in the awakened state. As you relax your body, you increase your oxygen flow, subsequently raising your vibrational frequency. There are many references available to assist in learning this process. Many offer a variety of exercises and techniques to help you find which method will work best for you. James Van Praagh's *Heaven and Earth* offers specific exercises, or if a workbook style guide is preferred, I suggest *Test Your Psychic Powers*, by Susan Blackmore and Adam Hart-Davis.

My abilities appeared through clairaudience and clairvoyance, and I also have the capacity to channel spirit. I hear the voice of spirit beings externally same as I would listening to someone on the phone. Sometimes I hear internally, which is a form of telepathic communication. (Telepathy is a skill where a person is able to read another person's mind, with or without permission. Being a medium is communicating to the spirit of the dead, not the living. A medium does not receive their message through the sitter; it comes through the spirit guides traveling with him/her.) I see spirit and energy fields the same as I see a person sitting across from me at a table. Sometimes spirit will provide still or moving images within my mind's eye.

I can 'turn on' my clairvoyant sight at will. To me, this is exactly like adjusting my eyes to see a Magic Eye 3-D illusion by N.E. Thing Enterprises. This is a computerized image embedded in an optical illusion art piece. To see the hidden image I must look slightly in front of the obvious figure and unfocus my eyes. Doing this reveals a 3-D picture. In the same way, when I want to see someone's aura I gaze above their shoulder or head, unfocus my eyes, and the aura shines out.

Within the realm of psychic abilities are multiple pathways of reception as well as a range of ways to apply them. How I choose to use my ability is not necessarily how another person will utilize his or hers; much like an artist. For instance there are intuits who can see sickness and disease (disease) like Carolyn Myss. She uses her gifts to help people understand the dynamics of illness and labels her ability as being a "Medical Intuit."

There are others who can see attached spirit in a person's energy field and perform a releasement like Irene Hickman and William J. Baldwin. On occasion I can see health related issues and attached spirit if need be, but I prefer to focus mainly on seeing and talking with spirit guides. I like to stick to the medium I know best and constantly strive to refine my skills.

Aura

An aura is an energy field around a person, animal, plant, or object. All things, both animate and inanimate, emit an energy field. In humans the colours of the aura are related to chakras located along the spine. There are seven main chakras, each about the diameter of a golf ball, positioned in exact locations between the base of the spine and the top of the head. These centers harness and move energy throughout the body.

Every human possesses the same chakras, but can make use of them differently. Each chakra is linked to specific organs and glands. Chakras react to the emotions and thoughts of the person inhabiting the body. These reactions in turn will relay messages back to the energetic body. This is how health and dis-ease are co-created. Whether you are happy, frustrated, or in love, your aura will mirror these emotions by changing in colour and shape. How you respond to the surrounding environment is reflected in your health. This is why it is important for your environment to be agreeable. At any given moment your energy field is adjusting to how you feel and what you think. To study more about chakras and energy read Barbara Ann Brennan's *Hands of Light*, Rosalyn L. Bruyere's *Wheels of Light*, or Ted Andrews' *Healing with Color*. Each of these books has brought me great clarity as I discovered the power of energy.

Although I can see dis-ease or illness being formed and any attached spirit, my main concern in viewing a person's aura is to assist me in knowing and understanding their personality characteristics. An aura reveals a person's physical, mental, and emotional traits, which make up their persona. In fact, it is colour-coded. There are many books based on colour theory, explaining how emotion is connected to colour. When I ventured into understanding this, I wrote down every researcher's results under its designated colour and compared the findings. In college I began doing my own research by writing down behaviors and colour patterns in people's auras. Based on location, proximity to other colours, and luminescence, I extrapolated my interpretation for the client. Now this is second nature to me.

Energy contained in an aura can move inward as if it is feeding itself, outward like the glow of a light bulb, it can have sparks or swirls, or it can even radiate downward as if a heavy blanket is wrapped around the person's body. Looking deeply, I check for any holes or dips in the energy field, which implies a physical injury or condition that is not functioning properly.

When I began reading auras I wanted to test myself. I found a St. Augustine man at a Psychic Fair who had a computer program that read vibrational levels around bodies. The program read them through a glove shaped piece of equipment imbedded with sensors. By sliding your fingers into the glove and staying completely still for a few moments the computer could print your aura, location of colours and a written description. I remember thinking, *Wow…I have only begun and a computer is already putting me out of business!*

I decided to test my skill by reading people silently before they would receive their printout. I had great success. Before the next customer, I told the owner what colours would be around her. After the fifth person in a row he told me, "I spent thousands of dollars on this computer program and you are able to do it for free. I envy you." This definitely boosted my confidence, especially because I do aura readings without the assistance of spirit.

In person, I start my readings by drawing the sitter's aura. It helps relax a nervous sitter and I include humor in my interpretations. When the sitter is more comfortable, open and relaxed the reading will have a clearer and easier connection. I draft the person's outline using chalks, which resemble a bowling pin figure with a rough duplication of the aura. I find it really difficult to match up colours. The colours I see in the energetic fields are much more vibrant than I can produce with chalks. After I complete the sketch I translate what the colours mean to the sitter.

A sitter, Leigh, came in for a reading on a late Friday afternoon with an important decision in her mind. After drawing her aura, and sharing the meanings of each colour, she was able to answer her undying question of whether to leave her husband or not before I even connected to her guides. She saw her patterns and understood her needs as a person.

I translated the colour meanings to Leigh while I wrote them down on the sketch. I began with the colour that was closest to her skin, which was mustard yellow. I instantly knew she was having an inner battle with herself about issues of love and respect, because the yellow was dark in colour and it was lying next to green (love colour). I explained to her to that she was mainly a logic person; she makes her decisions by analyzing and thinking them through.

Qualities like loyalty (blue, the third colour in her aura) are important to her yet there are dark green spikes in her aura interrupting the blue that showed me she was unhappy with these qualities. This was her pattern, always taking the right step as compared to by others, not wanting to hurt anyone else. She avoids guilt at all cost even basing her choices around it. I told her, her next decision should be based in love, to put herself first. This would break her cycle and create a wealth of happiness within her life. I also made clear if she were to do this it would come hand in hand with guilt, a feeling she was not happy to hear about. Her situation reminds me of Winston Churchill's saying, "If you are going through hell, keep going."

Being able to see a person's aura can also help to keep a balance between the sitter(s) and myself. I recall two women,

Sasha and Paula, who came together for a reading. Paula's energy was very unforgiving, like a walled up fortress. Her aura was muddy in colour, what looked like autumn leaves still hanging on a tree in spring. Interestingly the farther away Sasha got the less muddy Paula's aura became, which let me know there were issues between the two of them. I probed Paula to see if she was comfortable getting a reading with Sasha in the room with her. "I'm fine. I'm open to this. You do what you do," she told me. There were obvious issues between them Paula had not dealt with yet. The need to guard herself and keep secrets caused Paula's energy to shift colours, which blocked her from understanding and receiving information. She was too concerned about hiding her secrets that she was not allowing herself to be receptive.

Even though Sasha was open to receiving information, Paula would have blocked it for the both of them. I decided to give them readings separately. This made for a better experience for each of them. This way Paula could selectively share parts of her reading with Sasha without worry.

As for the theory of black auras being a precursor to death, this definitely does not ring true for me. I find truly negative, angry, or exceptionally imbalanced people tend to have dark(er) auras but after a body dies I have seen residual colourful energy still shining.

I was in a restaurant once and was seated next to a man who had a completely black aura. I did not notice it until my friend sitting across from me asked if I wanted to move to another table.

"Why?" I asked him.

"Because you are completely leaning over to the right — looks like you're about to fall out of your chair," he said.

When I glanced at the guy to my left I saw why. This man's energy was black as night. I told my friend I definitely wanted a different table. He agreed and got a table on the other side of the restaurant. By the end of our meal, the man had made a scene cussing and yelling at the young woman who was with him, shoving chairs around, and stormed out of the restaurant. It goes to show how energy is definitely an extension of actions.

Outline of a reading

When I give a reading I always open by giving thanks, saying a blessing, or offering a prayer. This is how I express my intent of goodness and honesty as well as gratitude for my abilities. Then I surround my client, the environment, and myself with golden white light for protection. I do this by stating it to be present. Thoughts and words are energy forms; therefore, what is thought or said creates equal patterns of energy around you. Know that "what you choose to believe in is your own truth."

Golden white light has a high vibration that creates a boundary and prohibits lower vibrational energies from passing through. This provides a space for spirit who are not invited to the session to stay at a distance. By using this method, I can clearly focus on the sitter. I teasingly remind my students to put on a spiritual white condom before beginning work. The shock of the word condom gets their attention and helps them remember to use protection.

When working with spirit beings it is important to know with whom you are talking. You don't just pick up the phone and dial a number and begin to take advice from just anyone. In my statement of intent I always mention the sitter's name and ask for their guides, angels, friends, and relatives to come and speak to me on behalf of the sitter's highest good and health. I also request any others to wait outside the perimeter of the light. Usually I say this to myself before the client arrives.

After giving thanks and stating my intent I open my eyes to a room filled with light and spirit. I work this way because my teacher, Marguerite, taught me there might not always be a quiet place to sit and meditate before the sitter comes or I may not have certain items I like to use to enhance a session. This allows me to always be prepared by needing nothing. I am able to work wherever I am regardless of the environment. All I need is my intent.

Spirit guides who arrive for the reading are the ones *willing* to participate. If there is a spirit being the sitter wants to communicate with who is not present, I will ask for their name and make a special request for them to join us. This will usually bring them forward. If the spirit does not come, I do not question their decision or speculate why they are not present. I understand there is a time and place for everything. Often a guide will come to be seen and not heard. Generally this happens to let the sitter know they are present, but do not have anything of value to share.

One time during a reading, a sitter's mother came through loud and clear. I remember her standing in the far back to the left. She was identified by her looks and told us how she crossed over. The daughter confirmed this. The mother said, "Well it is good to see you, I will let the others talk now." Ellen, the daughter was completely disappointed because she came only to talk to her mother. The mother then claimed, "Why would I waste your precious time. We talk all the time, especially in the car. You never get a moment to talk to Grandma. We'll catch up on the ride home." Ellen looked at me a bit embarrassed because she indeed had been having conversations with her mom in the car, but fearing she was a bit crazy, would not validate this to herself. Her mom did it for her.

Sometimes spirit will come to me despite my initiative, like in the Prelude. Clients will ask, "How do they know to come to you?" Well, when you have made a decision to be open to communicate with spirit a huge neon sign is placed over your head reading 'Open for Business'. Kidding, but

I do know spirit can appear to whomever when they feel it is necessary to get their message across. Spirit can do this through apparitions, auditory messages, feelings, or symbols.

The guides who appear for sessions are as real to me as any three-dimensional being. The only difference is spirit chooses how well defined their appearance will be by lowering their vibration which causes them to be more dense. When I see their 'body' standing or sitting in front of me, their image is transparent enough for me to see the furniture, walls, or art behind them, but adequately formed for me to see clothing, tattoos, jewelry, and even birth marks. Commonly spirit beings appear the way the client last remembers them or the way they were when they passed. But here and there, a spirit will show up looking the age they felt best when they were alive.

The first time I had spirit appear at the age of their choosing, I was living in a garage apartment in Gainesville, FL. I was just beginning to take clients. Until this point I had only done readings for my friends and family. I was feeling a bit nervous when I opened up my flimsy aluminum door to a middle-aged woman whose energy was locked as tight as a bank safe. I forced a grin and welcomed her into my studio. I motioned toward a chair at the kitchen table. Beverly seated herself and I took the chair directly across from her.

She began with, "I am a skeptic. I do *not* know why I am here. I do *not* believe in any of this. It is all hocus pocus."

"Good, I suggest you don't believe in this and remain a skeptic," I responded. The expression on Beverly's face was great; she looked completely confused. She was probably expecting me to hop up on a soapbox and defend myself or attempt to change her entire perspective, but that is not my job.

I spoke with Beverly about how I work and after asking her how to spell her name, I sketched her aura with coloured chalks. I told her what I noticed in her aura, breaking it down by colours and meaning by positioning as each related to her body. She listened silently. Then her father, a young and handsome spirit, entered the room. He stood behind her on the left side. First he explained how he died of a heart attack. He continued by detailing his service in the military, where he was stationed, facts about his wife, and all about his daughter's love life. Beverly's father was concerned and wanted to talk about her husband's affair. This was my first time handling this type of intimate information with a complete stranger. What if I was wrong? I decided not to mention it. I had no desire to be caught in between a struggling relationship. Her father was a real stickler and kept on the subject until he was yelling at me. Giving in to his persistence, I nervously told Beverly all the facts about her husband's activities outlined by her father. He explained receipts, phone calls, and a letter her husband was hiding in his sock drawer. He described the woman as being her husband's secretary and explained how long the affair had been progressing. There was a long moment of silence as Beverly digested the startling conversation. She seemed stunned I knew this information.

Tears of anger flowed as she exposed the particulars of how she already found the letter and seen the phone calls listed on the billing statement. Although she witnessed the physical proof, she was in denial. Beverly told me she wondered if there was any proof within the receipts and the day before our meeting she discovered the numbers on the phone bill belonged to her husband's secretary. To top it off, the father described the secretary to a tee.

After passing along all of these accurate points, my client denied the man talking was her father. "My father was an old man when he died. He looks nothing like what you are describing, and he never did." Her words struck me like heavy weights.

I asked her father if he could share anything truly

personal between the two of them that would help her to accept I was speaking with him. He asked me to thank his daughter for the little chocolate snacks wrapped in yellow she left him when he passed over. He opened both of his hands to show he held candy in them. I could not recall what kind of small chocolate bars came in a yellow package. I suggested Mr. Good Bar. Then Beverly described how at the funeral, before the casket was closed, she placed miniature Butterfingers in her fathers hands so he would have his favorite snack in Heaven. With this said the reading ended. She did not want to hear any more and continued to refuse the man in the room was her father.

Relief melted over me when she left the room. Her father told me she would handle the information well. "It was the confirmation about the affair she needed — not to understand it was her father talking. You did just fine. They won't all be like this." On that note, he left through the door after his daughter.

I received an apologetic phone call two weeks later. Beverly found an old picture of her father and she said he looked exactly like I described the day of the reading.

There have been a few sessions where before the reading started I got an overwhelming sensation not to do it, but instead of surrendering to the negative feeling, I overrode it and carried on with the sessions. After beginning I understood why I got those vibes. On two occasions the sitter had preconceived expectations of what the reading would be and if I wasn't following their presupposed agenda they became less and less convinced of the accuracy of the information or they believed it didn't relate to them. The sitter then gets to the point where they reject everything I say because it is not what they expected to hear or receive.

A long-time friend referred one person in particular. The reading was scheduled as a phone session and after our introductions it went as follows:

Several spirit beings arrived for the session and I thought I had judged my desire to not want to do the session too harshly. I'm thinking it will go just fine until the spirit on my far left tells me there are other people listening in on our phone session and the sitter is uncomfortable with this.

"John, am I on a speaker phone?"

"Yes, you are."

"So who else do I need to say hello to?" I inquired with a certainty of knowing this to be true.

"Oh well—my sister and her husband just dropped by; I told them about what I was going to do and they asked if they could stay."

"John, that is fine with me as long as you are comfortable with it."

"Oh yeah, they're family. I'm fine with it." He sounded all right, but I felt something different. I continued with the reading as an older female spirit gave advice on life and career—until John interrupted.

"I don't know who she is. This does not make sense to me, is there any one else there?"

"Be patient, maybe the information coming through now is in reference to times to come, a week or month from now."

He insisted this was not true.

"John, do you mind if I talk to you privately, I mean, can you pick up the phone?"

"Sure."

I explained to him what spirit was telling me. He had a smug attitude of 'well, if you're really psychic you can do this in front of any one.' I told him I thought it would be best to cancel the reading and reschedule for another time when he could be alone.

"I don't want to continue this reading when you are so certain that none of this pertains to you. I know your spirit guides are doing their best. The woman is repeating the same information she gave me to begin with and she obviously wants you to know it, but if this is not what you want to hear then it would be best to let this go. Call when you are ready to set up another appointment."

John has not called back—yet.

In situations like these, I never really know why the encounter turns out this way. It could have been John was put on the spot by his relative's request and couldn't say no to them. Maybe the information was true and he didn't want anyone to know it. Whatever the reason for this occurrence, John's reading was clearly not timely for him.

A private reading has its appeal. You have the option to receive messages which could not be received in front of others without having to worry about what is said or delivered. In group readings there is a silent privacy line the medium is aware of not to cross. As in all my group readings I now ask if the messages are too private for the company present to please raise their hand, I will write down the message and hand it to them privately.

Channeling

Spirit usually appear to me before the sitter arrives in person for their reading and this is when the decision is made whether the reading will include me channeling or staying to relay their messages. This is decided by spirit since they know if the sitter will be comfortable with this process. I have not channeled for anyone over the phone.

Before channeling, I need to know if the sitter is at ease with me leaving and understands how to handle the session. During my absence I ask the sitter not to touch me unless the spirit borrowing my body initiates it. By touching the channeler without permission, the sitter might startle the spirit. The spirit who is chosen to use my body is never there to harm, instill fear, or upset the sitter in any way, but if for any reason the sitter feels uncomfortable with the channeling all they have to do is ask for Jamie to come back. I tell clients they have full power to ask any question they desire.

The incoming spirit has to be granted permission by my gatekeeper (Granddaddy) before entering my body. This is a safety net devised to exclude any lower entity spirit from using my body while I am in a deep meditation. It is important for a channeler to lay down ground rules before letting anyone borrow their body.

Maitland, a nine-year-old spirit guide, on one occasion got into my chalks and drew on my face during a channeling session. She somehow convinced my client to promise not to tell me when I returned to my body. After the reading, my mother came over for a visit and asked me if I had been drawing.

"No, why?"

"Well you should look at your face in the mirror," she said.

I went to the bathroom and saw that Maitland had given me rosy checks, freckles, and a very large smiley face. No harm done but after this I made it clear my body was to be returned to me the way they found it unless they were healing a default in my energy. In a strange way I feel I am renting myself out like a car.

Many times the sitter's guides will channel through my body. This could be a spirit of any relation or a guide they have not met. Spirit beings are very excited when I agree to channel. Imagine…they get an opportunity to be human for an hour or two. Spirit get a second chance to feel heavy, to breathe (since breathing is not a bodily function in spirit form), to feel clothing against their borrowed skin, and experience physical touch.

For me channeling is like the fountain of youth. I cannot discern time while I am gone. A two-hour session feels fifteen minutes long until I return. Often when I am in the state of channeling I'm having a grand time exploring other dimensions or sleeping, a type of sleep where upon waking I feel refreshed and replenished. I don't recall things that transpire in my absence unless I knew before leaving or I received permission to stick around for the reading. This keeps a high level of confidentiality and also limits overloading my memory with all the facts and details of each encounter. Sometimes I feel like I get the greater benefit over the client because channeling is so much fun for me to experience.

It is more common for me to stay during a reading and translate what spirit says to the sitter. I basically become a secretary for my client writing their questions and spirit guides reply's word for word. I also document their actions and emotions; this way the personality of the visiting spirit can show through.

Asking Questions

One of the most important parts of a reading is the quality of the questions. Usually when I get into a reading the sitter will forget all the questions they had formulated in their mind. To circumvent this, I remind people to write down any questions they have beforehand. Any question is valid and can be asked, although spirit beings may not be able to answer if it directly interferes with the sitter's lessons.

Even questions about approaching or impending death have been answered. Whenever I am given a question or a message relating to death, my human side comes in and I get a little nervous. I tell myself to take a deep breath, leave my feelings out of this and connect to spirit. During one session, a sitter asked about a friend of his who had been missing for several weeks. Spirit gave the message that his friend would be passing on in two weeks time. His death would be his own doing because he would overdose on drugs, he would not be murdered. Spirit gave me a visual to where his body would be found. I explained to the sitter I was seeing a public place and somehow it was close to where I live. I named off a few streets just up the road. Then lastly spirit added, "The next time you talk with your friend will be the last. Be sure to make amends."

I was uneasy talking about someone's death who was still alive, but the messages spirit gave were so poignant and precise. There was no hints of maybe, or if. Spirit was talking very certain. It was eerie and peaceful.

Two weeks later I was rollerblading in Piedmont Park near my home with my dog and about the time I got home and took off my skates helicopters were hovering over my house. They were taking turns flying over the park to film the latest news. I somehow felt connected to this chaos. I ran out into the yard while my husband searched the T.V. channels for the news. A body had been found in Piedmont Park. I did not relate this discovery with the reading I gave weeks before until I received an e-mail the morning after from my client.

My client's friend called him early on Saturday. They talked for a long time about life, and how everybody wants him to be well. My client followed the advice of his guides and made closure with his friend. They said goodbye for the last time when they hung up the phone. He passed away that evening from an overdose. He was in the park next to the lake having his experience while I was rollerblading around it.

Another occasion where the time of death was indicated was with Denise. Denise came in to get a reading concerned about her ill mother. Spirit told Denise straight forward, "Your mother is going to pass over in the next few days. The next time you visit her in the hospital take with you your young daughter, not your son. Your mother will pass over in your presence." Spirit went on to explain about telling her daughter, Jennifer, every detail about her grandmother's illness.

Spirit told of how Jennifer is an emotional child. "She needs to hear and see all the facts about death to be comfortable with it. Denise, you will want to inform your daughter about every little nuance about her grandmother's health and about death. Even if you feel it is too much information for a young girl to understand, we need you to continue. This will allow Jennifer to understand the steps of death as being a natural process, and not allow her emotions to translate death as being full of anger, sadness, conflict and abandonment. The power of knowing will give Jennifer a chance to say good-bye, to make her grandmother's death a healing, and see it as a natural process. Her future experiences will be peaceful ones about death. Denise, this is a very important tool for Jennifer to have."

Denise went to the hospital a few days later escorted by her daughter. She explained everything to her daughter no matter how technical and explicit it was. Surprisingly to Denise, Jennifer understood all of it and now had a greater understanding of the process. Jennifer told her grandmother goodbye and was not afraid to let go. Her grandmother passed soon after, in their presence.

Overall, it is important for the sitter to know if they have a question, no matter how strange it seems, ask it. I will discourage them from giving me too much information and ask them to be clear and concise in their wording. The less I know about a sitter the easier the reading is for me. This limits my ability to interpret what is being said by spirit and keeps me from adding my personal thoughts or opinions. This does not mean the sitter should be non-responsive to the messages he or she receives, this actually helps the flow of conversation.

I find many people presume spirit to be all encompassing, all knowing and unable to make mistakes. Overall when a soul makes a transition from Earth to Home she retains the personality she built during the life on Earth combined with other lives her soul has experienced. Progression is cumulative. Material possessions get left behind but knowledge compounds. Spirit will carry over the same traits, be it an encouraging personality or a cautious approach to trying new things; yet, they will have a greater overall perspective of life. Although the spirit will not possess anger, hatred, suspicion, or the need to have power struggles, they can feel sorrow, discouragement or even unworthiness. These are types of emotions that would not be imposed upon any other spirit because they are personal expressions of themselves. I experienced this through a particular session with Emily.

Emily lived in a clean neutral-coloured condo. I positioned myself on her overstuffed white couch and prepared my energy for the reading. First to arrive was her father and he came through clearly. He stood to her right side facing me and before he could speak he was crying. He begged for forgiveness. I told the woman her father was present. I explained how he died, what he looked like, and the strained relationship between them. She acknowledged all this to be true.

Her first words were, "I don't know why that bastard is here, if he is going to talk I do not want to do the reading. I have nothing to say to him."

Well, I understood why he was crying. The daughter refused to talk to him or forgive him for his actions on Earth.

I explained to Emily how her father was upset and apologizing for harming her. "You need to understand when your father died he was able to understand why he did certain things. He is telling me he acknowledges his actions were wrong, but at the time he didn't comprehend that. He understands you are angry but was hoping for a few minutes you could set that aside and look at what he is trying to do now."

I sensed for the first time in Emily's life her father was behaving like a responsible parent.

"Well isn't that a little late," she snipped back.

The father again tried to repent and do his best to smooth over her abusive memories of him. She wasn't giving him the time of day.

"That man raped me whenever he wanted. He got what he deserved. He rotted in jail. Why should I ever forgive him? I am the victim here not him."

With this said I knew the reading could go no further, she was not ready to listen. This was her father's cry for peace, which would not be heard by Emily that day. I packed up my belongings, thanked her and left.

Emily's desires about having the reading included questions about love, career, and life in general, not about rehashing her relationship with her father. One of the nice things about this reading was how Emily's guides stepped aside and allowed her father to come through. Her guides knew planting the seed for forgiveness might create an opportunity for healing down the road.

In other readings, I have been privy to a newly passed mother, filled with grief, apologizing to her child for leaving. Although I have seen spirit express emotions; I have not witnessed a spirit project a lower level vibration or emotion onto anyone else, human or in spirit. Spirit beings share their feelings; yet, contain the emotions that need to be worked through. They are as human as you and I in many ways—minus the physical baggage.

Ending a Session

When the session is over and spirit has said all they feel is important, we all say goodbye, thank each other for the shared opportunity, and I give the written notes to my client to take home. There was a time when I tape recorded the sessions, which was much easier than writing, but I stopped because I received many complaints from clients about not being able to hear my voice over all the others talking. They heard laughter, or every other second would be blank, and sometimes the entire tape recorded silence. Even testing the equipment before the reading to be certain it worked properly didn't guarantee a good recording.

Spirit is notorious for messing around with electrical equipment; i.e. televisions, radios, lights, telephones and more. Maybe they go the extra mile to interfere with equipment to leave their mark with the client.

It is for these reasons I went back to writing notes for clients. This way the client gets to see all that has been said during the reading. I do not keep any records of readings because I feel each one is the property of the sitter. I am extremely strict about confidentiality. A reading is very personal. If I ever share my learning experiences with family or friends I will use alias names and places.

Phone Readings

While living in New York City, I was seeing clients at their home or apartment. My guides kept me safe by informing me which readings to go to and which ones to cancel. Gratefully I always had pleasant experiences.

The day arrived when I received a phone call from a woman named Rachel who was desperate for a reading. She received advice from two different friends to contact me. She had the most beautiful voice and perfect enunciation. Not what I expected from someone living in Boston. Everyone I knew from that area had a heavy northeastern accent. Her geography certainly wasn't revealed in her voice.

"In Boston?" I asked, "Well, are you coming to the city any time soon? Because I don't do phone readings."

She impressed upon me how she had to see me and questioned the possibility of me doing a session over the phone. I told her to call me the next day at 4 pm and I would try, but no promises…and I would not charge her.

My phone rang as soon as the clock registered 4:00pm. The time was right but there were no spirit guides at my house waiting to talk to her. I tried pleading, giving thanks, and saying prayers to get spirit to come. Nothing. I told her I was sorry and exchanged polite conversation about the weather.

As I paced the apartment slightly frustrated, I plopped onto the edge of my bed. Looking around I saw…seven people standing in my bedroom!

"Oh my God! Hold on, they're here!"

The man in front began talking fast, explaining he was her husband. Pointing to his ears he teased about an ear game they played. He said she was about to buy a location and laid out the contract with all the accounting information she would need to make it happen. He even included legal advice.

Rachel fully understood everything and was very excited. Her husband kept giving details about the location she was to own the next month. He mentioned the two adjacent buildings where it was situated in the city, as well as a description, but something concerned me. I never want to make assumptions, but all the spirit beings in my room were dark-skinned with an African American appearance. They spoke with a rhythmic speech pattern that this woman had no trace of in her voice. I slowly explained their appearances including their skin tone.

She was humored by my cautious description as she laughed, "Yes, Jamie I am a black woman! "

Although I felt embarrassed, her lightness brought total relief.

She disclosed she is a famous radio personality and the location is not only an office space, but also a location [frequency] on the radio dial. Her husband had described the office building from where the location was to be purchased. Since he was an accountant he dictated all the necessary paperwork to complete the process. Rachel received more information than she hoped for and I triumphed over my inability to do phone readings. It was a great experience for both of us!

What I once thought impossible now made perfect sense to me. Spirit understand our linear world and are able to travel to any location when they are needed or requested. Spirit are amazing and this is proof to me of how they will accommodate our needs and constraints in this physical world. Phone readings have now become a daily occurrence in my practice. I give the reading the same way as I would if the sitter was in front of me, with one exception — I do not draw their aura.

Lessons and Discoveries

"It is not a matter of building up the awakened state of mind, but rather of burning out the confusions which obstruct it. In the process of burning out these confusions we discover enlightenment."

–Chogyam Trungpa

Spirit enjoy reiterating to me, "The only limit in life is knowledge. As soon as you decide to stop learning, you have decided to stop living." I have heard this repeatedly from guides since my childhood, as well as in many readings. This is the secret driving force behind my love for reading books, attending workshops, and teaching.

Another reminder is, "What you choose to believe in is your own truth." The depth of this statement is endless when I think about it. Whatever a person believes, will be the truth to them and it may or may not ring true for the next person. I have always believed in equal values and fairness, so this teaching took me a while to truly understand.

In Gainesville I took a six-week psychic course under the instruction of Doug Davis, a mystic. He emphasized the power associated with people's abilities — I found this repulsive to the umpteenth degree. Power? Isn't that a bit macho? My beliefs knew power as an external force, something used to manipulate. I believed power was what governments had over cities by maintaining laws and enforcing social conduct codes. I didn't relate "power" as a facet of communicating to spirit guides. At the time I knew psychic abilities as being soft, feminine in nature, and gentle with respect to others and yourself. My definition of power didn't match Doug's viewpoint so I rejected that part of his teaching.

In the years to follow my truth shifted and the fundamental nature of power crept into my work. I found I needed a balance of masculine and feminine in my readings. My constant soothing energy needed to be able to translate the hard-edged messages for sitters. Doug's definition of personal power being psychic power in time became mine. I often wish, in my youth, I would have given more attention to other people's teachings which contradicted mine. Not necessarily accept them, but keep them in the back of my mind as possibilities. My truths changed with time and experience, bringing me the understanding to not be offended by other people's beliefs; they could very well become my beliefs some day.

To be or not to be...

Crossed over, kicked the bucket, six feet under, become food for worms, moving on, changing states, metamorphosis, going in, entering the pearly gates, transitioning, birthing out, exiting, pushing up daisies…what ever you call it, it is definitely an end, opening a way for a new beginning.

Many people assume it is easier for me to handle death because I am a medium. I have had multiple experiences with close friends and relatives passing on. The physical removal of a person's presence, the day-to-day absence, takes more than clairvoyance to get accustomed to.

There are people who never get comfortable with the loss of a loved one. The hugs, touches, phone calls, sitting around the table chatting or watching movies together – these reminders are ever present and do not necessarily fade with time. I'm not removed from these feelings of loss although they are softened by the reassurance I gain from knowing I have the potential to see and communicate with them again. There are no guarantees as to how or when, but I can at least check on their arrival and state of being through other spirit and if need be offer my assistance.

One More Time...

Spirit have told me that before returning to Earth, we choose our life lessons and the family who will create an environment to achieve these lessons. Spirit counselors help each returning soul to map life lessons that are reasonable and potentially not too overwhelming.

"Reincarnation is a choice, not a punishment," Grace, a spirit counselor, tells me. Grace is a well-educated British woman who is very proper in her vocabulary and dresses to the nines (always in white). She has thick blonde hair that falls straight against her cheeks. Her job is to help people write goals for their next lives, to assist in choosing families, and to plan interactions. With the incarnating spirit, she strategically helps plan out the exit points in their life to go along with lessons they would be learning during the specific age range. Grace is quick to say if you have too much on your plate at any one time. She keeps a record on all of the "children" she watches over.

I first met Grace in Portugal while channeling for a group of people. The friends that gathered around were some of Grace's children. Her interaction with them was motherly in a personal and global way. She attended to every person individually doling out messages and answering questions, not once hesitating. Grace's teachings to her Portuguese children about being reincarnated together before reminded me of my first proof that souls recycle. `

One Friday night I was looking for a movie to rent

from Blockbuster. I was a sophomore in college so by now I had seen all the movies in the place until I came across a video which was going to help me discover my past lives through meditation. I thought it was strange that Blockbuster carried self-help spiritual tapes, nonetheless I rented it. I was well into Marguerite's private classes and interested in discovering new ways of meditation.

I put in the VHS and laid down on my couch. The visuals were all psychedelic with swirly colours, very nineteen sixties in style. There were no specific images on the screen at all. A man's voice came over the patterns and used a relaxation technique similar to hypnosis to guide me into a deepened state. He then guided me to open my mind's eye and to describe what I saw. This is when I began to see a farm; the green rolling hills in the distance, the fences made from tree trunks creating horizontal patterns around a two story barn keeping the horses in. I walked into the house nearby. The floor was made from compacted dirt with some stone in certain rooms. I reached around the room to touch any items; I was interested in exploring this environment. I knew I was lying on my couch yet I felt completely present inside this new body.

When I was guided to the climax of that life by the voice from the tape, I was lying in bed giving birth to my son. My midwife was there and her name came clearly to me, Samantha Anne. She had long thick wavy blond hair and beautiful blue eyes. She was exotic-looking, for southern Italy. Samantha was from Sweden, and had met my parents during her travels as a young woman in northern Italy. She stayed with me when I moved with my husband and became the town's midwife. This was my first and only child.

The following memories came quicker as the voice guided me to the end of that life, to the moment when I was to die. I was running out of my home towards the barn. Samantha was pacing frantically in front of the barn doors.

Flames had burst out of the doors when I arrived. I cried out to her, "Where is Ramon?" With one look I knew he was in the barn, playing like he always loved to do. I cut around Samantha and ran through the flames. There he was curled up on a patch of hay. When I reached him, flames had engulfed the entire barn. I could not see where to turn to leave, and the heat was physically draining. I placed Ramon under me and curled my body over him. Knowing if I could shield him from the fire that I would burn and he would live. I believed whole-heartedly that Ramon would live. Meanwhile we both were bathed in flames. The last thing I remember is squeezing Ramon tightly, and then we were both released.

By now the voice on the TV was directing me to return. "Coming back into your body now, you will remember everything."

This was my second introduction to Samantha. The first came when I was on the floor in my bedroom begging for the voices to disappear. I was having my break down and a woman came to me saying, "You're ok, I love you." This voice did not introduce herself then but waited eight months to be able to share her story with me. She was none other than the woman I saw as my midwife, Samantha Anne. She stayed with me for several years teaching me how to mediate, eat better, and how to receive and deliver messages. Samantha was my first guide that I had met, worked with, and created a deep friendship with. She was in essence a best friend until one day she announced to me that she would be leaving. She had taught me all she could and now her time is approaching to reincarnate, but not to be upset, I would see her again. When she left, I definitely had a feeling I would meet her again, I just thought it would be the next day, as usual. But I did not see her for about one year.

During my stint of college I babysat off and on for the Head family and soon became their nanny. When I began working daily with the Head family they had just welcomed a baby, the youngest of four. The parents had all sorts of names picked out for boys and girls. The mother had a home birth and as the story goes, the baby was a little girl and after holding her all the names they had chosen did not seem to fit. The mother had a name come to her when she was holding her baby and decided it fit her child perfectly; hence they named her Samantha Ann Head. At first I thought nothing of it, until I saw her. She had the same blue eyes and blond wavy hair.

The children and I connected instantly. I could not have had a better job. Every afternoon I would pick up and chauffer the kids to piano, football, violin, singing, dance, YMCA, and other countless activities. Afterwards we enjoyed doing homework, going to the parks, and talking about life. The children grounded me and kept me alert to reality, they were such a blessing.

When Samantha was about three we were coming back from dropping her sister off at dance and she asked me straightforward, "Jamie, do you remember when we used to ride horses?"

I almost drove off the road trying to look at her. She was in the back seat staring out the window, unaware of me being shocked. She continued talking to me about the life we had shared so long ago.

"I miss doing that. We used to ride everyday and I took care of you."

"I miss it too, Sammy."

"I know who you are, Jamie," Sammy's voice depicted a wise woman, not a three year old.

"Of course you do Sammy and I know who you are too."

"Jamie, I love you."

"I love you very much too."

My heart fell apart inside. She really was Samantha Anne. Here she was reborn into a family where I was already connected. If I had not had the whim to rent that video tape years before, this conversation might have slid right past me and I would not been reconnected to the first person to teach me to believe in myself, in my own strength.

Often during my channeling sessions I am able to recall memories of any lifetime I have experienced. By channeling it gives me the space to explore or simply take the time to rest (which I mostly choose). Meanwhile back with Gracie, she was in deep conversation with her children. After her channeling session, lasting about four hours, I was introduced to her playful yet serious ways of presenting messages through the many stories from the people in the group. The most intriguing to me was how she speaks with a perfect high class British accent.

Stop this Ride, I Want Off!

While planning lessons for an incarnation a soul inserts several exit points, allowing for choice over when to leave. An exit point is the moment when death is permitted to enter in and give a person the option to cross over. Grace confirmed we could have as many as nine exit points. How ironic, cats have nine lives too!

You may not be consciously aware of when an exit presents itself, but know when one comes up you either consciously or subconsciously make the choice to act upon it. Opportunities like a car accident, a slip and fall, a near-drowning, getting cancer, having a heart attack, surviving a lighting strike, et cetera, can all be potential exits.

Recently my husband and I had a severe car accident. It was a rainy day when Rui was at the wheel driving us back to Atlanta from our visit to relatives in Florida. While traveling around 65mph in the middle lane of I-75 North, our SUV hydroplaned. The Four Runner slid towards the metal median strip. Before hitting the center barrier, time seemed to slow down, my awareness heightened and in that moment I looked at Rui and calmly said, "Relax, we're going to be okay." We heard the metal scraping across the asphalt as glass shattered and popped. It was an eerie experience. After three flips and several spins that sent us reeling across every lane of the northbound highway, we landed in the fast lane facing oncoming traffic.

It still baffles us how we didn't hit anyone and no one hit us. The policeman who responded was surprised to find us practically uninjured. After following us to the local hospital he shared how when he received the call he was certain he was going to be "pulling bodies." Never had he seen a person survive a wreck the magnitude of ours. Rui scratched his finger and I hit my head a few times, causing an intense headache. The doctor diagnosed me with a bruised brain. Other than this, we were in working order. Needless to say, the SUV was totaled.

No doubt, I was shaken up over the experience and no longer take driving in the rain lightly. Thankfully, my dog Madame Blue, who always travels with us, was left in Atlanta with my brother for the first time. Had she been in the car, I am certain she would have been thrown from one of the broken windows. The concept "There are no coincidences," was again confirmed for me.

When Grace came to answer my questions about the accident, I gained clarity on what had spiritually happened. She explained at the moment I told Rui we would be okay I verbalized my desire for us to live. In doing this Rui focused on his quest for life. This was all spirit needed to know to keep us safe through the ordeal. Grace reminds me that I am not the only one affected by my choices. In other words, upon my recommendation, we made a choice to stay on Earth. This was an exit point we chose not to take advantage of. I've heard it said humans learn best through experience, but what a way to learn about exit points!

An alternative way of looking at soul mapping and exit points is comparing life to a trip to Disney World. Pretend you are traveling with your family and friends to Disney World in Orlando. First you must have a ticket (the desire to reincarnate). Next you decide what rides you will ride and what you want to see based on what time the shows start (you choose lessons, times and places to be to learn them). Now, even though you might have only chosen three rides to ride, you can go ride other ones (freewill), or choose to the ride the same ones over and over again (some people go through lessons without learning them, so they repeat them until the lesson is understood while others choose to ride all the other rides and hold out for the ones they really want, to save the best for last).

If you were to miss the midnight parade you would have to wait until the next night to see it, same if you miss the monorail to Epcot, you will have to wait for the next one (if you deviate from your personal goals or lessons in life and "miss" opportunities that would have supported them, then you will need to wait for them to reappear in your life). Waiting can be short, like for the monorail or long like when Space Mountain was under construction.

You allow yourself to invite four friends in addition to your family. You choose wisely and carefully and your decision is based on the criteria you have created. You understand at any given moment you might have to void your decisions to help these friends and family members with their own lessons, or you might choose to isolate yourself (you chose a family and friends to help support the lessons and goals you choose, whether positive or negative).

All great trips consist of some planning. Most people set up a meeting spot at a certain time, the Haunted House every hour on the hour, if you get separated from each other, or decide to split up (planned meetings with other souls). But just like any day, if you are not aware then no matter how hard you look for them at your meeting spot you will not see them (this is all about freewill).

Now, the final action is to decide when to leave. Would you leave Disney, after traveling all this way, before you rode all the rides you wanted to? You can always leave the theme park and drive away; no one is holding you there. You may decide the weather is not what you expected and leave early (suicide), or ride all the rides you wanted then leave (partake in an exit point), or decide to only complete one lesson then leave, in hopes you will come back another time to complete what you did not finish (use of reincarnation to help complete lessons). But most likely you will leave when you are good and ready.

As abstract as this little story is, it has clarified so much for my sitters when I explain the terms of mapping, freewill, destiny, and exit points.

For me, I was able to learn a few new facts from Grace about the process of incarnating. I am intrigued not only by how we map situations into our lives, but by how we weave exit opportunities to be considerate of freewill. Grace also very exactly clarified the one exception to exit point planning—suicide. This is one choice that is not an exit point and is not written into a life map. Suicide is an act of freewill.

Suicide

Have you ever known a guy who is physically coordinated to where he can play any sport well, treats everyone like a friend, and greets everyone with a sincere hug? — An all-around genuine good guy. This was Donnie, a close friend to my brother and me, who took advantage of his freewill and chose suicide. Donnie reached a point in life where words were not enough to express himself and he thought action would be better. He substituted a gun in his mouth for his inability to communicate his frustrations to others. His transition took place in front of his girlfriend. I was shocked when I heard the news. I knew Donnie was not the type of person to harm anyone, let alone himself. Deep inside, I wanted to believe it was foul play. He was my first friend to cross over.

About three years after his transition Donnie came to me in spirit and explained everything, detail by grueling detail. I was overjoyed to reconnect, saddened to hear the true details, and enlightened to receive insight into how his suicide plays out in his afterlife existence.

When he passed over he explained to me, he instantly felt he made the wrong decision, but there was no returning. His body was too damaged and could no longer sustain life. He observed his girlfriend's reaction before being pulled from the scene. A force grabbed him from behind and placed him in a room without walls. Here Donnie saw his life speed by him in a 360-degree panoramic movie theatre. While watching the scenes play before him, he felt every emotion each person in his life experienced as a direct cause from his actions. Happiness, pain, sadness, joy, jealously and more surged through him. When his movie ended with his death, family and friends who had passed on surrounded him to bring comfort and familiarity.

His next step was to see the counselors. They were in a conference-like room seated behind a crescent shaped table. They reminded him about the basic law of cause and effect. What was to happen with the rest of the life he did not live on Earth? What was going to happen to the people he would have come in contact with if he remained alive? The counselors told Donnie he would have to contact all these people while in spirit and continue to give of himself, in the same way he would have if he were living. Overall, Donnie did not remove himself from his problems. What he assumed would be an escape turned into a new level of responsibility and action for him. He added a full afterlife of counseling and intervening. Now he is completing the work he would have done if he had chosen to live out the rest of his life.

Donnie informed me there is no one direct path a soul follows every time after choosing to take their life. The road one takes after death is directly based on their beliefs when they were alive, therefore, a soul can end up a Lost Soul, in the Healing Space, Home or other dimensions. I decided to bring up a commonly asked question, "I heard all suicide souls reincarnate immediately, is this true?"

"Reincarnation is not something you do quickly unless the trip has already been planned for you. Most the time we are, I mean souls who choose their passing, are in need of help or counseling, so we are assisted to heal before we return. There are souls who come here through choice of suicide that are healthy. Yes, Jamie, that does mean suicide is not always a negative action. "

Donnie told me when he passed over it took several Earth years to adjust to his rash decision; thus, the reason for it taking three linear years before he came to talk with me. It was time for me to accept that his passing occurred from nothing other than his act of freewill. I miss him in his physical form and I am forever grateful he came back to explain himself. I have since healed from our separation.

Often healing comes through reconnecting with spirit, especially when they can bring us clarity, information, or details on the reasoning behind their departure. This is exactly what happened for a sitter of mine named Jerry when he came seeking answers to a friend's questionable death. He came by my office for his appointment with a list of questions in a notebook. Jerry is a forty-odd year old man who looks much younger than his age. He sat on the floor with me while I delivered the messages I heard from a spirit named Brian. Brian had recently passed away and he felt it necessary to unfold the mystery related to his own death. He needed his friends and family to be at peace.

The reading went as follows, written in Jerry's words.

"Jamie relayed that Brian fell from his balcony. He was tending to something using the rail and lost his footing. Then she spoke as if Brian were talking, "I fell, I fell, I fell, off backwards...I lost my footing. My foot tried to catch me, but I fell. No foul play. They took me before I hit the ground. I was fixing the plants and stood on the small rail, (she draws the railing) turned and fell over backwards. It was after work, into the evening, after sunset. I saw city lights but it was not dark."

Brian's body was actually found in the Chicago River after he fell from his balcony on the 34th floor. His friends and family had been questioning what took place that ominous night and were wondering if his boyfriend could have possibly been involved. They considered whether there had been an argument or a fight.

I asked her if drugs were involved, as suspected. Jamie said yes, but not serious ones. I asked her about 'K'. She said yes, 'K'. [Special K is a drug that produces a small high and can alter your equilibrium. It is used as a cat tranquilizer by vets and has become a popular club drug.]

When comparing this information with his close friend, I found out the police questioned the boyfriend. He [the boyfriend] went into the kitchen and when he came back Brian was gone. He knew Brian could not have left the apartment without walking past him. He guessed Brian might have been trying to get the cat or take care of a plant. He told them that they had sniffed some 'K' earlier.

When I visited Chicago after this reading I saw for myself how the balcony rails were vertical instead of horizontal (just like Jamie had drawn), and the explanations fell into place. It happened just like the boyfriend had reported to police.

I passed the information from the reading to friends in Chicago, who then explained it to the family. Everyone felt a sense of validation about what happened to Brian. Initially his family wanted an investigation into the boyfriend; however, nothing more was revealed. Thanks to the details supplied by Jamie, Brian's family and friends have resolution to the matter."

Mirror, Mirror on the wall, predict my future, details and all.

When looking at the possibilities of future events it is wise to consider freewill. I personally enjoy questioning spirit about the future. It works for me because I understand future events change with every moment. When spirit gives details of the future and a time line, it may not play out exactly in the way described. This is due to freewill and choice. You may make a decision that changes the outcome of the event foretold to you. Future is not a fixed destination. Spirit replies to your future question by looking at where you are in the "now" moment and formulating how you might behave in the moments to come, thus creating a possible future.

A great example of this was in February of 2002, when my spirit guides told me that my boyfriend was going to propose to me in March. Even though I knew we were traveling down the road to a stronger commitment, it was a surprise to hear of the immediacy of action.

The way I behaved, after spirit guides told me the month of the proposal, is how accurate the information turned out to be. If I had kept quiet, I would have had a beautiful surprise.

Unbeknownst to me, my sweetheart was planning the whole thing. But seeing how I cannot keep secrets from him, I told Rui the revealing news. He was calm and never let on he had been contemplating any plans. I thought about the news daily like any woman anticipating fiancée status would.

I was scheduled to take a cruise with friends the final week of March, and Rui wasn't going with me. In my mind this would have been the perfect chance for him to ask me, to confess our commitment to one another before I jaunted off to the Caribbean.

March came and went without the question. We were in the first week of April when I began thinking he was not going to ask me. Then one unsuspecting evening, he proposed. At the tail end of his romantic request he informs me, "I would have asked you in March but you were always talking about it and I wanted it to be a surprise."

When future information is given use it like road signs on a highway, letting it guide you. Do not make it the map to your destination lined with expected refueling spots. Remember, even roadways are under constant reconstruction.

Groupies

Through the years I have given readings, I have had some spirit guides return to me with different clients. I learned this is related to "soul groups" or "soul families." The same as we have families here, we have families in spirit. Groups of spirit beings travel together throughout incarnations. Within a soul group a number of spirit beings will choose to reincarnate together and the rest will stay behind to help. The ones who do not incarnate can be spirit guides for those who return to Earth. It is this reason some people will have spirit guides in common; they are in the same soul family.

Several members of a soul family will frequently travel together; these are called soul mates. Yes, I said soul mates—

plural. One soul mate could be in spirit, another incarnated as the opposite sex or the same sex, one may be a family member, and even still another could be someone else's child. Soul mate does not necessarily mean the one you will marry and live with happily ever after.

You will know when you are in the presence of your soul mate; there is an undying connection that will present feelings of familiarity and often an unexplainable level of comfort. There is a magnetic force between these souls because of the soul family connection; what once was together will want to be together again. They can draw out the most passionate of feelings from within you. Even though all of these incredible feelings are present when soul mates reconnect, you and your soul mate(s) still have the potential for what is perceived to be an unhealthy relationship. In soul families each individual is willing to participate in any role needed in order to facilitate your learning experiences here on Earth, whatever these may be.

When you reincarnate with another spirit in your group more than any other, that soul is your twin flame. There is only one twin flame in your soul family. A twin flame connection goes beyond immediate levels of comfort and attraction into sharing the same feelings, thoughts and dreams, as almost if the two of you are one. Each reincarnation together forms a bond. The easiest visual I can think of relates to telephone wires. If one wire (one reincarnation) gives you a good line of communication, imagine what a hundred wires can offer. Two souls would be able to communicate on many different levels.

The telephone wire metaphor brings me to a good story to share about one spirit in particular who travels with several of my clients, as well as me, Maitland. She works with multiple soul groups simultaneously, guiding hundreds of adults and children. She maintains the image of a nine-year-old girl even though her last incarnation ended in the

1930's. Maitland, her mother, and her baby brother passed over together during a car wreck in the snow. She always likes to brag how her family was the first to own a car on her block. Maitland decided that she liked how a child could communicate more easily and innocently to adults; therefore, she decided to remain at a young age. She also made a conscious choice not to return to Earth and to continue living in spirit form. From this state she can help children retain their memories of Home and assist adults in remembering their intuitive abilities. She was placed with a mentor named Saint Michael to study for her next position.

Maitland was with St. Michael for several of our years before finally earning her "wings" in 2001. She was off and running after that helping as many as possible. Grace informs me wings are a term for a distinguished level of mentoring. This meant Maitland no longer needs St. Michael's guidance. Even though she brags about her pearly set of feathers I rarely see them on her. She likes to look more human, "it makes people more comfortable," she confided to me.

I first met Maitland through Marguerite during my initial experience witnessing a channeling session in one of her private classes. I remember Marguerite had me sit at her left side. I think she was prepping me. I was nervous and wondering if I was too close to Marguerite whether my soul was going to get dragged out with hers. Maybe it was a silly thought but when you are experiencing something new in the spirit realm your imagination can get the best of you. As the spirit was exchanging positions with Marguerite I could feel the pull in the room. I gripped my white plastic chair and began encircling myself with energy from my head to the floor in order to ground myself so I would not fly away.

The next thing I remember was Marguerite speaking with a deep heavy accent like she was from India. A new soul had arrived; he was a Master teacher and spoke very distinctly. Everyone watched in awe as Marguerite's body stiffened to match the voice. The energy shift in the room was trancelike: intense, and heavy. He passed along information to each person individually, and offered general knowledge to the group. Nearing the end of his time he began to get irritated with another spirit that wanted to come through and speak with us. He kept saying, "She is not able to come through, there is not time."

Then, for some reason the spirit beings switched positions inside Marguerite and out came a giggle. Immediately this spirit rearranged Marguerite's body by pulling up her legs and crossing them in her lap. She spelled her name loudly M-A-I-T-L-A-N-D, over pronouncing the D. Then she began to sing How Much is that Doggie in the Window, first and second verse — she knew all the words. Her singing lit up the room.

I remember looking at the other people in class wondering if this was real. Maitland explained that the Master spirit told her if there was time she could possibly come through and speak to the class, but if she did not have anything to say she would have to leave....so she sang. She knew there was not enough time and she was too young to give advice, but she loved every second before the other spirit beings talked her into leaving Marguerite's body.

When Marguerite returned, the members of the class explained how Maitland rearranged her body. Her face went stern; I had never seen Marguerite firm before. She thought we were teasing her. She went on to explain that she has metal pins in her hips and they do not bend that way. It is impossible. She even told us we could talk to her doctor if we did not believe her. I had no idea Marguerite had this procedure done. I searched my memory to recall if I had ever seen her sit on the ground. No, she always sat in a plush chair with armrests. This was Maitland showing us impossible really means "I'm possible."

Now that we know Maitland, let's get back to the

telephone wire metaphor. Maitland uses the following imagery to teach me how "God", soul families, and telepathic skills are designed to work. I believe this will help show a different possibility, kind of broadening of the perspective.

First she likes to confirm that BellSouth is the largest server for my area. (I agree with her even though I really do not know for sure.) Then she begins her story, "Pretend that God is BellSouth but he could not call and talk to anyone because there were no other factories and telephones were not invented. Okay?"

"I am with you so far Maitland."

"Okay, then God decided he wanted to know himself better so he helped create an environment that would support telephones. So when telephones came about they could call him, and he could know himself, because all souls on Earth, like plants, animals, insects, and humans are bits of God's soul."

"I understand. You are telling me that God created life with parts of himself but evolution of life gave us the knowledge of creating a way to communicate with God, who is in essence ourselves."

"Yeeeeesssss! But that's not all. BellSouth set up factories all over to help people get connected. Then other telephone factories set up shop like MCI and Talk America; these other main factories are heads of religions. So if you were to sign up with one of these factories you would be using religion to get you in touch with God."

"What if I were to use Bell South?"

"Bell South is another path to God, but because it is the original inventor you would be in charge of your own service, like spirituality. See?"

"I think I do, go on."

"Okay…so not only do you have a telephone connection to God, you have a telephone connection with all things living. You can call anyone you'd like; this is what you call telepathic skills. You all are all connected through your souls. But wait there is more! You even have calling plans, where you choose a certain amount of people to put in your calling group, and this is your soul family. And what is so neat about that is that your soul family does not have to all be under the same server. Get it?"

"Completely. You are saying that all living things are connected by telepathic abilities because our base makeup is of the same origin; God. And soul families can be composed of all different backgrounds and beliefs. Our connection to the members of the soul families depend on how much time we have experienced to together, causing a stronger bond and communication."

"You got it! So you can see how soul mates and twin flames are created and how they can be very different from you, even in beliefs. So does BellSouth make it easier for you to understand the basic layout?"

"Yes it does Maitland. I am grateful you can take an everyday action and compare it to the entire spiritual world." I definitely understood more about the workings of soul mates and soul families as well as God's role but I like to test everything I am taught.

In the overall view, Maitland is considered a mentor. There are more roles that spirit fulfills like counselors, guides, and teachers who can travel with several soul groups at the same time. Maitland has found herself in several person's readings doing her best to make us all laugh with her childish humor and great singing voice. She has an amazing ability to bring a blanket of comfort to the room by using her odd metaphors.

Before we move on to other topics I feel it best to end the chapter with a firsthand experience. Ashley, a 30-year-old psychology student living in Marietta, Georgia was curious about her romantic soul mate and Maitland was willing to oblige her request for information. Ashley's reading is a great example of how spirit handle questions of soul mates.

Ashley arrived on time for her reading. We both sat on the floor of my office in the sunlight. She had a million questions on the tip of her tongue but I told her to hold off. I had a feeling I was going to be channeling the session and I needed to explain what was about to happen to Ashley. She was very understanding and extremely excited for the opportunity. I began my channeling and the following, in Ashley's own words, was what had aspired.

A little nine-year old girl channeled through Jamie. She told me who she was and said her name was Maitland. I asked my big question first, "Who is my soul mate?" She said I was going to meet a guy on a trip after the summer. She said this trip would be far away in a place that is like "God's country". He will be muscular, with dark hair and have a focus in his eyes. She stated that she saw books surrounding us and that we will have a learning center in common. We will also both like to engage in some type of physical activity and that this will link us together. She also said that if I didn't go on this trip that I will meet him soon after the first of the year. She then proceeded to tell me that this man is not "the one". But I have to meet him in order to find my soul mate.

Later that year for Thanksgiving, my family and I planned a trip to Lake Tahoe where my parents planned to renew their wedding vows. At the last minute we cancelled our plans and went to Vegas. In February of 2000, I was at the gym working out when suddenly I saw this man that I had never seen. He was a personal trainer that had just started working there. He was absolutely gorgeous. He had dark hair, dark eyes and was very muscular. I could hardly look at him because he had this forceful stare in his eyes. I observed him for a few days then finally introduced myself. His name was Austin. We talked at the gym for a few weeks and then he asked me out. We got close very quickly. One night over dinner in casual conversation we were talking about where we had gone for Thanksgiving. He mentioned that he and a few friends had gone to Lake Tahoe. I asked him the exact dates and he told me the dates that would change the way I looked at him forever. I reviewed all my notes from my reading. He is the one I am supposed to be with, I thought. (For right now at least.)

Another hint was Lake Tahoe has a nickname of "God's Country". There was no doubt in my mind that Austin was the one Maitland was talking about. We met at a type of physical activity (the gym), and as far as the learning center and books surrounding us goes, we attended the same college. I began to feel like I was on the right path. Unfortunately, I could not tell him what I had learned. Austin did not believe in any of this. If I had shared this information with him he would have called the whole relationship off. Needless to say, we didn't connect spiritually. The only problem was I really liked Austin and I was aware that he wasn't "the one." But I knew I needed him to get to my soul mate. In March I went to a barbeque with Austin and met his friends. When one of them named Johnny approached from the sidewalk I gasped for air. I felt really guilty because I was so attracted to him that I showed Austin a lot of attention that day.

Austin and I dated for about two months then decided to call it quits. After the break up I immediately began asking about this guy Johnny. I couldn't get him off my mind since meeting him at the barbeque.

The weekend after the break up I went to a club with friends, which were Austin's friends too. Guess who showed up? Yes, Johnny. He came to the club because he heard I was there. I was so excited and I couldn't wait to get to know him.

We started out as friends and realized that we were in fact soul mates. I recognized that Johnny was the reason I met Austin. The little girl from the reading kept saying I would meet "the one" through another guy. Well, Johnny and I were married on August 2, 2003. The experience of this reading was life-altering. If I didn't have the information from the reading I would have tried to make it work with Austin and wasted a lot of time. I also would have been devastated thinking another guy had disappointed me. I know I would have met Johnny sooner or later but the messages that I received from the reading brought me peace of mind about my future, my past and my current situation.

Chapter
— SEVEN —

Things You Always Wanted to Know, but Were Afraid to Ask

"Our deepest fear is not that we are inadequate. Our deepest fear is that we are powerful beyond measure."
—Nelson Mandela

Friend to friend, if we were sitting in my living room our conversation could be more candid but for the most part people don't get the opportunity to ask these types of questions. Out of my personal curiosity I've done it for you. Like my Aunt Carol says, "People want to make it [mediumship] complicated but it isn't, that's the confusion." Here is the lighter side of the work.

Do you mind…Can I get a little privacy here?

Ever had a suspicious feeling like someone is watching you while you're doing a little private something like picking your nose in traffic, using the toilet, taking a shower, or better yet…having sex? Is this your subconscious, or is someone really watching? Could it be your deceased grandmother?

Countless times I have asked the question, Do spirit watch us [humans] while we do our private things? I would like to say they would never watch us while we engage in that sort of activity but the answer is yes and no. No matter what action you can come up with, regardless of how private it may seem, it will not affect the way spirit perceives you, even if the spirit is your relative. Spirit beings understand the beauty of being human is discovery. When spirit sees you are approaching a private moment they will most likely leave you because they're not needed.

"I can not recall a time where anyone was in the midst of passion and asking for my advice, it is preposterous," Grace announces in a channeling session.

Pressing further, "Well? Does spirit watch us?"

Grace answers me for the twentieth time, "…You must understand your personal hygiene and sexual behaviors are not a highlight to us. These actions are purely human and should be enjoyed. We do not judge you for what you do with your life. We have respect for your choices. We are not intrusive. This would make you uncomfortable."

I finally arrive at the conclusion: if you are comfortable with having spirit around at certain moments they will arrive.

One time I was taking a shower with the bathroom door closed and I heard the old door creek open. I knew it was my husband. Sometimes we will discuss the day's events while I shower. After a few moments of silence, I peeked around the curtain. I was stunned by who I saw and nearly slipped on the side of the tub. Lo and behold — there sat little Maitland on the toilet lid swinging her feet and staring at me.

"What are you doing Maitland?" I asked, sure there was a good explanation.

She replied so innocently, "Watching you."

"Well then, I bet you noticed I'm taking a shower. Isn't this one of those private moments I ask about?"

"Well…yes, but Rui watches…" she replied looking up at me, "and I don't mind you showering."

I informed Maitland of the difference between my husband being with me while I shower and her stopping by to chit-chat when I'm in my birthday suit. My rebuttal was not too persuasive.

"Nudity is natural, Jamie. It is the same as looking at you with clothes on," she says. She stayed with me talking up a storm about anything she could until I finished. As soon as I turned off the water and pulled back the curtain, she was gone, leaving the door wide open. "Ummm...hello? Maitland...do you live in a barn?" A chilling breeze after a warm shower was not what I desired.

Do spirit beings make whoopee?
Yes, spirit beings have sex, but they call it merging. This is when two spirits allow their energy to completely merge with each other creating one form. My spirit friend Donnie says it is the most incredible feeling, but both parties involved must desire it.

"Imagine being completely vulnerable and honest with another person and when you go to kiss them your lips fuse together," he tries to relate the feeling. "You are allowed to feel every emotion contained within the other person even if it is a lower energy. You completely permeate each other... hence merge."

Donnie tells me it is stronger than the greatest physical orgasm you can fathom because it saturates every part of your soul.

Will this persuade one to believe in an afterlife? If the idea of eternal life doesn't do it, maybe the idea of eternal sexual bliss will.

Calling all spirit...Calling all spirit...
Ouija Board, pendulum, dowsing rods, crystals, Ruins, Tarot, tea leaves, coffee grinds, colour cards, or playing cards are all tools to assist the user with their gifts. Tools are a great way to begin your journey into the psychic world. They help build the confidence needed to trust intuition. The trust you give yourself will be reflected in the accuracy

of the messages. Eventually there will be a point when a person becomes equally accurate without the use of tools. Sometimes people transfer responsibility for the answers or messages onto the tool instead of owning it as information coming directly to them. These mechanisms can be fun as long as they are used properly. Stating an intention before using any instrument for spiritual contact is important. Intent, also called blessing, prayer, or protection, is an acknowledgement of purpose in the activity. It can also be used to clarify with whom you want to communicate. When stating my intention I am clear about my willingness to work only with beings of the highest energy for my highest good. If not, I potentially open myself to beings of lower energy.

Michelle, my college roommate, and I once used the Ouija board without properly saying our intent. A spirit came though the board and started spelling out messages for Michelle — horrible, shocking messages about her sister having a car accident and being left to bleed to death. Then the spirit went on using curse words directed at both of us. When the "f" word came across we agreed to get off the board, clean it, say a blessing and demand all lower energy beings leave the property at once. None of the messages given to us that day on the board came to fruition.

Negative souls do exist. What would the positive be without the negative to balance? These souls usually live In Between. The soul that came through the board obviously wanted our attention in any way possible; unfortunately he resorted to lower tactics. Because he didn't allow a civil discussion, we had to stop communication and were not able to help him.

Generally spirit can only do harm if they are somehow given permission. The slightest fascination or curiosity from humans is enough to keep the spirit's interest. It is up to the individual to set the rules. Cases where spirit beings attack unwilling participants are few and far between and should be handled immediately and delicately by contacting a medium or priest. It is a good idea to use someone you are comfortable with. Human beings have more power over the contact of spirit, ghosts, and paranormal than they may realize.

When the act of using a tool is complete, saying goodbye or thank you will close off contact. Also, claim responsibility for the answers received. By using a tool, a person is saying they are ready to receive messages from spirit, with or without devices. Please be careful and responsible with these methods—these tools are more than mere games.

Once I had rediscovered my dad's Ouija board and practiced receiving messages on it with Michelle, I brought it home on one of my college breaks. I was nineteen at the time and well into Marguerite's classes. I wanted to show my dad what accurate information was coming through on the board, with proper intent, to see if he had the same experiences before. Instead, Jane, my step-mom, was more interested. She was more than skeptical, but was really curious "to observe us with the old time parlor game." We thought it would be better if she asked the questions while we received the messages on the Ouija. That way we would all know no one was cheating. Her experience changed the way we perceived the board. Here is how our evening went as described by Jane in her own words.

"I thought I would see what they would do if I asked them questions about my deceased sister, Kathy. Kathy had passed on in 1983, five years before I ever met Jamie or her father. I had never mentioned to Jamie having a sister who died. Much to my amazement the validation—questions, birthdays, etc. were answered accurately. Then the most amazing thing started to happen. Kathy began to answer my questions, through the girls on the Ouija Board before I spoke. The girls were puzzled because their fingers were perched on a piece of plastic moving around spelling out answers to questions they were not hearing.

To top it off, this apparently amused my sister to the point where she started to giggle by spelling out the word, then outright laugh by pushing the plachette over the picture of a smiling sun on the board. The girls told me this means the spirit is laughing. This is when I realized her personality was showing through the fingertips of my daughter!"

So tell me what spirit really think about humans?
One afternoon, as I sat at my computer working, I felt the need to know how spirit view certain human concepts. Like a Sherlock Holmes of the spirit realm, I began poking my finger into my guides' faces, demanding answers. Because I was prying, spirit metaphorically pulled up a soapbox and a microphone and proceeded to give me a piece of their mind—I started typing. What I heard was not the funniest or sweetest response, but it rang true to me.

First topic: RESPONSIBILITY.
Grace began, "Humans are obliged to show responsibility for their own life. Responsibility for the actions they take upon themselves and upon each other. Most humans do not understand that their thoughts alone are a form of action."

"Understanding this," Grace continued, "the action of thought creates their environment. We see most humans believing they create their environment by the psychical actions they do. They can be as sweet as apple pie on the outside and inward have the most wretched thoughts. Believing, since they are nice, they will receive the same in return. However this is not true. Once thought is created it spans outward much like the ripples in a lake after tossing in a pebble. The quality of the thought is what is returned to the person." She paused for a second. "You are looking at me quite blankly, are you typing or listening?"

With an emotionless tone I told her, "I am listening, I swear, I just thought you were going to say something encouraging."

"Am I misunderstood? Did you ask for encouragement or truth?"

"Truth," I confided.

"Allow me to carry on, as for responsibility…most humans create situations where if they were at fault, they would have room to place blame on another element of the equation. They are not likely to see themselves being at the center of the blunder. Humans in general are mentally lazy and do not want to look at themselves too deeply. 'Ignorance is bliss' tends to be their motto. This way they do not have to correct their faults. They are choosing weakness over power. Responsibility needs to be present in all actions humans take or it is not complete."

If I had a tail I would have stuck it between my legs, but I understood why they were speaking this way. Generally, we humans are unaware of our own ignorance. There is so much more we can utilize energetically. Our society runs rampant with the show of external power. I cannot wait for the day we match it with internal powers of compassion and true love. Materialism thrives while our true authentic power sources are barely tapped.

Topic number two: KARMA.

My tail may have retreated, but my curiosity didn't. I needed to know more. Pushing on I inquired, "So tell me about karma. This word is casually tossed around in our society. I have heard things like, 'Oh, that's bad karma,' 'I could feel her karma,' or 'Karma will pay him back.' Shall

I go on with the karma sayings?...'We spend the first part of our lives repaying karmic debts' and what about how—"

"In Home the word karma does not exist," Grace again took over. Her face was calm and assured. Her British accent is so distinct. "Humans created the word karma to explain the unfortunate mishaps which occur to good people. Karma also fulfills the need for revenge. When a terrible deed is done unto a person, karma can give false satisfaction for the person believing karma will come back and bite the perpetrator."

Grace stepped aside as Maitland added in her nine-year-old lingo, "You know it's true! Thoughts are like throwing a boomerang. What you say, do, or think goes out into the universe and will come back to you, but you better know it comes back ten times greater. Even though energy is a boomerang, it will not create its own identity...Poof!" she said, gesturing like a magician making flowers appear out of thin air. "...and seek out revenge as the word karma can suggest."

She paused many times, taking deep breaths for effect, "If...there is...left over energy...from past lives...which causes an individual...to live life in a punished way, it is because it was chosen and written into the life. Guess what?"

"Chicken butt." This made her shrill with laughter.

"No, I'm cereal." (Meaning she is serious.)

"Okay, what is it Maitland?"

Maitland straightened her posture. "There is no payback you have to make from a past life. Because it is taken care of in the life review process just after a soul passes...and... lessons learned are reviewed with your counselors because you can finish a lesson at Home, you don't have to be on Earth to complete anything. There is no deadline!"

"Deadline? Maitland, this is funny," I told her.

"No silly, I am talking about karma. There is no revenge

on the spirit side, you do it all yourself." She smiled showing all her teeth. "Okay, Jamie, next topic!"

"But wait! Why do we reincarnate if we can learn all our lessons in Home?" I felt I had opened up a really good can of worms.

"Jamie, you come back because you want to. Really, life is very simple. You can learn your evolution in what ever dimension you choose. No one pushes anyone to achieve lessons by reincarnation. Duh, it is fr-"

"I know: freewill. I get it. Next topic!"

Final Topic: The concept of DESTINY

"Why pray if life is predestined?" I questioned.

Grace's expression showed she was brimming with desire to reveal her response. She moved closer to my ear preventing me from seeing her face. Her voice sounded heavenly, "By expecting all the elements of your environment to work together harmoniously, you are consciously giving up all power of freewill. Jamie, you must understand this all goes back to responsibility."

"Grace, what about me—someone who does understand responsibility, are you saying I shouldn't pray because I know what will be will be? Is it 'life is what you make it' or —"

"How bored would you become if every decision in your life were made for you, allowing the most positive outcome without any effort or input by you?"

"I would be extremely bored. Is this a trick question?"

"If you were to believe destiny is fixed then you are not participating in your life. I will do my best to put this in simple words…" Either she could still see my face or she sensed my confusion and continued, "The concept of destiny is like the cruise control systems you have in your car. You set the speed and the momentum carries you through no matter if the road is under construction or freshly paved. As the driver, you decide how smooth the ride is by steering into or around (the road hazards) or even choosing to remain on the road at all. Destiny is a driving force that can be altered by freewill."

"I get that. I really do, but what do blessings, prayer, and affirmations achieve for people in everyday life situations? I know thought creates energy and we as humans can control our health this way. We are in control of our bodies but we are not in control of other people's lives, thoughts, actions.... here is where I become a by-stander, right?"

"You may have lessons and exit points prewritten within your lives but there is not a step-by-step guide on your day-to-day life." Grace came into view as she moved around to face me, causing me to stop typing.

"Praying, setting intentions, your affirmations and meditating all exercise your freewill and offers evidence to your spirit guides and your God that you are being proactive. This shows you are participating in your life; you have desires and a direction you want to travel. You may also send helpful blessing to others to guide them in their day-to-day situations. Jamie, not only are you responsible for yourself, you are responsible for others and prayer gives you the opportunity to do this. We are all connected together."

"Okay. When I pray for someone, I am sending him or her thoughts of energy that can help their situation. Like sending an encouraging e-mail from computer to computer? It's like refueling their tank, right?"

"Very well put."

"Thank you, um, if you don't mind I think I am done asking questions now. I am really grateful for your answers but I don't want to overflow my tea cup. Plus I need to get back to working. Thank you, guys. Until next time." I ended our talk. Maybe I will pick back up the role of Sherlock Holmes but I know now, I really need to be prepared for an intense conversation.

What scares a medium? Seeing dead people?

Although I've been clairvoyant for many years, having surprise contact with spirit beings when I am unsuspecting still gives me a fright. One evening I fell asleep on my living room couch and in a groggy daze decided to make my way to the bedroom. A man in spirit appeared before me as I rounded the corner from my living room. Instantly I was spooked. Stepping back from him, I called to Rui for an escort past the bathroom and into the bedroom.

"I'm not going alone," I told him.

"Jamie, why would this one scare you?" He seems to think I am nuts.

This one happens to be our house spirit. I talk to him, but he doesn't respond and it makes me feel uneasy. It leaves me uncertain as to why he is there and I would be more comfortable if I knew the reason for his presence. Until he and I reach a common ground and communicate with each other, I will continue being apprehensive and let him intimidate me. Silly considering the things I have encountered, but everyone has their weakness.

My least favorite way for spirit to present themselves is what I call the "floater." These are spirit beings who appear to hover over me, especially when I'm lying in bed asleep. I have opened my eyes and seen a spirit's face right in front of mine. Ever wonder why ghosts float in scary movies — because it really happens! Like most people, I enjoy the polite distance people maintain when conversing with others, and I prefer to have the same distance when talking to spirit. But when they pull "the float," they are right on top of me, which is too close for comfort.

On a more serious note, another haunting facet of being a medium is receiving negative images. During the fall of 1990 there was a serial killer preying on petite brunettes at the University of Florida campus in Gainesville. The murderer would follow the victims back to their apartments, where he would commit the crimes. My boyfriend at the time actually moved into one of the apartments where a double killing had occurred. Because no one else would rent it, he got it for a discount. He also believed it was the safest place to be, reasoning that the killer wouldn't commit a crime twice in the same location.

I was extremely uncomfortable spending any time there because I picked up images of the rape, suffering and the brutal murders that took place. These visions were accompanied by the loud music the murderer used to muffle his criminal actions. Bits and pieces of imprints (energetic remnants) about the victims flashed in my mind; these still sit in my memory. I never initiated contact with the victims, since it was too close to my personal fears and I didn't want to confront them. The perpetrator, Danny Rolling, was caught several months after this period. He was tried and sentenced to death for taking the lives of five university students.

These same personal fears keep me from doing police and detective work. Once I was asked to do psychometry with a piece of evidence to help a criminal case. Here I initiated contact with the missing person; it was unknown if she was dead or alive. While holding the piece of evidence, I went through the ordeal suffered by the missing woman. It was as if I were her, reliving the struggle for help and fighting for life against a rapist and a large knife. I was deeply frightened by the pain and tremendous fear she felt.

The experience was overwhelming, and this is why I choose not to do police or detective work. Although I cannot set aside my fears in order to give an in-depth reading for such circumstances, I am very grateful and respectful of the mediums that can. I know it can be tough.

You Want to Keep it Light or Enlightened?

Massage therapy still is a viable career for me, as long as my clients know it is my Clark Kent job. I know longer hide my abilities from any of my clients. They see the carefree side of me and like to send me comic cut outs and e-mail me jokes. Nick, a massage client of mine who is an attorney, brings numerous puns to my Clark Kent job. He likes to tell me when people he knows have died. Eventually I asked him why he found it necessary to tell me the obituaries during every massage.

He responded, "Well, you are the corpse whisperer. I thought you might know some of them."

I laughed but it is not quite the title I would use. I have learned to be lighthearted about my abilities because a dose of humor can help the digestion of nearly unbelievable information. I'm not sure if I would have signed up for this career out of high school if I were presented with a detailed job description. Imagine, standing in line to register at a University and I turn to the person behind me to ask, "So, what are you majoring in?"

A handsome bookworm replies with, "Oh, I am taking Psychokinesis with a minor in Séance to round it out. And you?"

"B.A. in Mediumship with a minor in Channelling," I confidently respond.

In comparison to more traditional occupations, I don't think mediumship ranks high on the success ladder. And, I couldn't imagine putting that on my resume or a job application. Have you ever seen an advertisement in the want ads reading: 'medium wanted, 30 hours a week, with benefits, needs experience or will train on sight'?

Out of fun, I have designed a prototype for all aspiring mediums in order to accurately depict what is needed in this role:

Job Description of a Psychic Medium

1. Mediums will never know what he/she is getting into until in it, which can easily be compared to stepping in dog poo. A lot of good can come from it; you can find out it is actually mud, a twenty dollar bill can stick to your shoe, or maybe your shoe was really dirty and now you have a good reason to wash it.

2. A thin line will separate the reality of the visions received and the reality of daily life, often leaving one with a slightly imbalanced feeling. If you do not recognize this is a true ability then you get to try out a lot of calming medications like: Prozac, Valium and Xanax or herbs such as: Happy Camper or Kava Kava.

3. At times, being a medium will challenge the three "F's": your fears, your family, and your friends. Caution: People will think that you need to take the drugs listed above but remember we are talking about an ability not a dis-ability.

4. Mediums can be subjected to odd experiences, at all hours of the day, in order to be presented teaching material for self and others. Note: This is not a nine to five career; your sleep hours are approved by spirit to be working hours.

5. Must possess a healthy body, mind and soul to become a good conduit for spirit's messages. Bye-bye cigarettes, alcohol, caffeine, and M&M's. Say hello to wheat grass.

6. Candidate must be a good listener. Number six really means what it says.

7. An understanding of the true meaning of responsibility is required. You can forget about sharing your days with co-workers and having office parties. You now work for yourself, unless

you are fortunate enough to find a company who hires psychics and meets all ethics.

Now I have informed you on the job requirements, are you more lightened or enlightened? Bringing the funny stuff along helps, but I am here to share my experiences for one reason: if only for a moment, however brief, you suspend or broaden your beliefs of the afterlife, I will have achieved success in bringing this material to the public.

Unlock your doors people; it's safe.

Part III: Personal Accounts

As a medium I have performed countless readings and I enjoy the many interactions connecting living people to persons in spirit: some family, some friends, and many complete strangers. The wonderful opportunity this career affords me is that no two days in my life are exactly alike. There are similarities in the lessons people learn, but my day-to-day routine is never scripted. I have a unique life, a unique ability, and I am blessed to be able to share it with the world.

Of the sessions I have been involved with, there are a multitude that still come to mind as "miraculous," "wow," or "oh my gosh," eye opening experiences. I wish I could share them all—verbatim—with you. Instead, I have opened the door for my clients to bring their story to you firsthand. This provides those who are comfortable exposing personal details a platform to share and it gives me permission to present my side of their interaction.

Getting in Touch with Your Other Side

By Joey Reiman (Founder and CEO of Brighthouse, LLC.)

Most of us are fond of having another side. Steely-eyed executives regale in giving their friends a peek at their human side. Kind people love when others notice their iron side.

Sexy, it seems, to have two sides, but this is not what the duality of man is about. There are no sides. Good and Evil are one. Abraham Lincoln used to say that we were both good and bad. All that mattered, he said, was which part won out.

Lincoln would have loved Jamie for two reasons. First, because her good wins hands down, and second, because she might have prevented his assassination.

Jamie is a psychic medium who truly has two genuine sides, human and non-human. Her earthy and earthbound side is both delightful and insightful. She is quick-witted, full of whimsy and highly intuitive. This is where her other side gives her a wonderful advantage.

Jamie has the god given talent of talking to those who have passed on and would like to share vitally important messages back to the people they cherish.

Through Jamie, I was able to talk with my dad who went on ahead back in 1982. Also present was my great-grandmother, whom I have not seen since 1959. Oh, I didn't see them that day either, but I know they were there.

Through Jamie, now-distant relatives and teachers shared stories with me that I can't share with you here. Each is either too personal or too precious. All are precise, though.

Yes, Jamie has taught me that we have another side, but it's not inside of us. It's out there. Her reading showed me the writing on the wall. And it was wonderful.

Thank you, Jamie, for getting me in touch with my other side!

–Joey Reiman

Chapter
— EIGHT —

The Circle of Life

"We are the mirror as well as the face in it."

–Rumi

Many people have communicated through me on the subject of children. Most often it relates to whether they will have a child, when they will conceive, or when the baby will be born. On a few occasions the topic has touched on miscarriage and abortion. Spirit amaze me with the ease and simplicity they use to approach these gentle topics. Grace, in particular, comes to discuss these issues.

"You must understand," Grace begins, "the reincarnating spirit already knows if their new body will make it to full term or not. If the body will not make it, the soul will travel along side the mother's body until that time occurs, or the soul will have a choice of incarnating into the small body for their personal lesson of loss," she says.

Every time a spirit has approached this topic through me to the sitter, the incident of a miscarriage or abortion has happened. Spirit is very aware of what to convey in order to minimize the shock of receiving this type of news.

Through the pendulum, spirit told my pregnant stepsister if she were to have any bleeding during her current pregnancy to go directly to the hospital. We used the pendulum (a six to eight inch string with a weighted object at the end used to answer questions psychically by swinging in certain patterns) because she did not want me talking directly to spirit in front of her and we were sitting at a booth at Dairy Queen. I held the crystal pendulum over my hand while it answered all my questions: Will the baby be full term? No. Is the baby healthy? No. Will my sister have a miscarriage? Yes. Will my sister's health be in jeopardy? No. Should she go to the hospital if there is any sign of a miscarriage? Yes. Is there a certain sign she should look for? Yes. Is it cramping? No. Is it bleeding? Yes. Would this mean her body is trying to abort? Yes. Does the baby know what is happening? Yes. Will she have other children? Yes.

Looking back I can only imagine how much I freaked out my stepsister. At least throughout our little question and answer session we knew spirit was more concerned about my sister's well being. They were not trying to scare her but inform her.

A few months later she had small signs of bleeding without pain, remembering the advice she went to the hospital. The doctors told her she was in the process of a miscarriage and she was able to receive the care she needed to heal properly. I am forever grateful her health was protected. Since this experience she has given birth to three sons; during each subsequent pregnancy she did not ask about contacting spirit to check the status of the baby.

These types of readings offer me proof of spirit's knowledge of souls traveling to Earth. They talk about the child's history from previous lives and can even pin down any medically associated problems before birth. Spirit can offer information about the pregnancy, birth, the unborn child's personality, and appearance. This is what Baba did for Veronica. After nine months I enjoyed hearing the details about the baby and how the information from the reading was confirmed.

Baba Gives Confirmation
Veronica, 29, Sales Consultant, New Jersey

In March of 2002 my husband and I went on a cruise through the Caribbean to enlighten our spirits and attend workshops with James Van Praagh and Dr. Brian Weiss, M.D. This is where we met Jamie. John and I were surprised when she eventually told us about her clairvoyant ability. She didn't look or act like a psychic. (Whatever that means!) In the past I have never gotten a reading because I felt superstitious and was a bit suspicious of what a psychic might say. However, after talking to Jamie I became intrigued by her skills.

My first reading with Jamie was over the phone in June 2002 and lasted about two hours. During this reading my grandma (mom's mother) and other spirit guides came through. Jamie told me my grandma, Baba, is my main spirit guide who always assists me and looks after my well-being. In this life she took care of me when I was a baby. It brought tears to my eyes to know she continues to look out for me.

Baba kept making references to "the baby" during the reading. So Jamie said; "You are either pregnant or you will be pregnant very shortly." What Jamie did not know was I had used a pregnancy test a day earlier and it showed I was pregnant. Talk about validation! My Grandma explained I would have an easy pregnancy, would gain 38 pounds, would crave soups in the beginning, and that the baby was a boy. Although Jamie was told the sex of the baby, we have decided to wait until the birth to know.

I am now in week 31 and so far she has been right. I've gained 28 pounds to date and I have had a "kickback" kind of pregnancy. Surprisingly in the middle of the summer I was craving soup!! In addition, my Grandmother told me to go to a chiropractor to have my L2 vertebrae checked. Following her advice, I went and my chiropractor, without reference to any other problem, told me my L2 vertebrae needed adjustment. I could not believe it. Jamie was accurate with every detail she told me.

My husband joined in toward the end of the session. His father, Norm, came through. It became very emotional for us; we were in tears. His Dad described an incident that happened right before our wedding in June of 2000. He recounted the details of a night when we were with family outside our summer home in Mays Landing, N.J. We were gathered in a circle talking as our family gave us their wishes/blessings before our wedding. During this time no one was inside the house and only one light was left on in the kitchen. Whenever I looked into the house, I would see a shadow going back and forth by the window. John saw the same shadow. At the time we had a feeling it was John's Dad since he had built this house and his ashes were scattered into a nearby river. Through Jamie, John's father corroborated this experience and told us he was with us that night. It is so reassuring to know spirits of loved ones continue to be with us, even after they have passed. It gives me much hope in life and hope for the afterlife.

The reading experience for me was extremely emotional, spiritual and uplifting. Afterward I felt like I was walking through clouds for days. It's the best

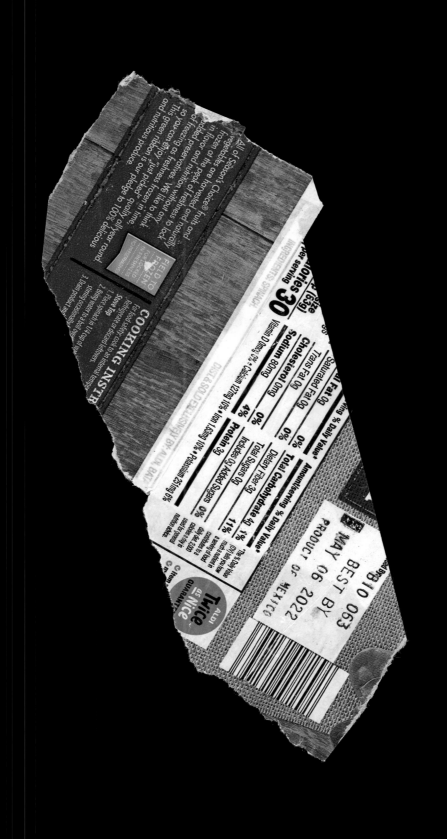

form of therapy. "Jamie's spiritual therapy," is what I call it.

Last, but not least, I would like to leave you with a message we received from John's Dad: "Life is short, learn to LIVE in the moment...it's only life after all!!

Update: John Jay Jr. was born in February 2003

Love and Peace,
Veronica

"Does everyone talk to their dead grandma?" a close friend inquires. "I've watched those shows on TV and it seems like everyone talks to their grandmother." It might seem like most people speak to their deceased grandmothers, but masculine figures come through too. Remember, females historically play the role of the nurturer and caregiver, which brings an emotional intensity to these readings.

I helped my friend understand the forming of close-knit relationships in soul groups. Those spirit beings who choose to be in our physical families have strong ties with us. Often members of the same soul group take roles as relatives and due to chronology, grandparents tend to transition back to the other side before grandchildren, which allows them to aid us from the other side.

Grandmothers are great for many reasons. They give unsolicited advice on love, career, and homemaking, pass on lost recipes, and sometimes even help find lost objects. A sitter named Erica connected to her grandmother during a phone reading. Her grandmother came through very strong. She gave me a "you are talking too slow" look; for a second I thought she was going to take the phone out of my hand and talk to her granddaughter herself. She told Erica, in her melodic Jewish rhythm, about a small broach (a broachlette is what she called it) in a box on the top shelf of Erica's mother's closet located in the bedroom. It was an item she wanted Erica to have.

Erica responded to her suggestion with, "My grandmother didn't have a lot of jewelry and I believe all of it has been passed out to the family already." Erica didn't recall any jewelry that looked like what her grandmother was describing. The grandmother did not take Erica's doubt lightly and I intervened by telling Erica "it would be fun to look anyway." A few weeks passed when I got a phone call from a very excited Erica.

"Guess what I am wearing right now…my grandmother's broach! It looks just like she described it! My mother had forgotten about it and found it in a shoe box in the closet." I was pleased to hear she was able to fulfill her grandmother's request.

Another grandmother described how she appears in physical form as bubbles in order for Deanna, her granddaughter, to know when she is present. Deanna recalled a few photos where bubbles appeared above her daughter's head and sent me a copy of one taken in her living room. The bubbles in the photograph glowed; yet, they had distinct edges like soap bubbles, very different from light rings that can show up on photographs.

Often grandmothers have played memorable roles in the sitter's life and by returning to communicate with their loved ones they can help solidify or foster a belief in an afterlife. It's wonderful these spirit beings choose to remain in contact with family members.

Numerous grandmothers have connected through my sessions; some come to say their hellos then move on, others are dominant spirit guides of the sitter and provide a wealth of insight and information. William happily reconnected with his grandmother who sparked him to travel across the Atlantic Ocean in order to trace his family's lineage.

A Little Clue Here and There
William, 40, Attorney, Atlanta, Georgia.

Jamie was nothing like I had expected. She appeared to be in college or had just graduated. Yet, her eyes glistened and twinkled in such a way that I knew she was special.

After sketching my aura with colored chalk, (which was all very nice and interesting, but not the reason I was there to see her), she glanced around the room with her finger pointed as if she was counting pictures on the wall. It turned out she was counting the spirits present in the room.

I have always felt a special connection to my mother's side of the family, who came to the United States from Germany. In particular, I have a bond with my maternal grandmother even though she died when I was six years old. I never understood why, but everything about my grandmother, her parents, and her six German siblings intrigued me. I have always wanted to know as much as I can about them, which led me into the area of genealogy.

It turns out the feeling I have had all my life is true: my grandmother is one of my guardian angels. She has been carefully watching over me and monitoring my life. Through Jamie, she related events and observations that nobody could have known had they not been privy to some of my more personal moments.

I do not remember everything discussed during my first session, but one statement stood out. My grandmother at one point said, "I have had to learn how to be strong here," (on the other side). This made sense to me; my grandmother committed suicide because she had difficulties dealing with the problems of life. I have always heard that we are put on this earth to learn various lessons. What we do not learn or fail to learn while on earth, we must learn when we cross over.

Suicide is not the evil damning event that many religions make it out to be. However, suicide is not a good thing because it artificially cuts off our ability to learn what our souls need to learn. For some reason, which I do not completely comprehend, it is much easier and more beneficial to learn the lessons we are supposed to learn while we are on earth.

The messages and statements made in my sessions have been confirmed over and over again. To relate each and every aspect would not only be too personal, but monotonous; however, one particular promise made proved to be a personal validation and a priceless gift. Needless to say, my grandmother was the architect of this.

I had been planning a trip to Europe. One of the places I was going to visit was the charming medieval town in Germany in which my grandmother was born and where she spent some of the happiest days of her life as a child. During a session with Jamie, my grandmother and other relatives could not contain their excitement over my trip. My grandmother said (through Jamie) when I visited her hometown she would be giving me a gift each day I was there. I remember thinking, "it will be interesting to see how she pulls *THAT* off!"

I really was not thinking about my grandmother's

promise during my first hours in her hometown. I walked the cobblestone streets and took in the atmosphere of this incredibly romantic place. At one point, I walked into a bookstore where I encountered an elderly gentleman who I assumed was the owner. I chatted with him a bit using embarrassingly broken German I had learned in school. I must have mentioned to him my grandmother and her family living in the town. He instructed me to go to a certain building where I realized my ability to speak German was pretty pitiful. I interpreted what he said as I would see some old photographs of the city if I went to this place. I guess he saw my struggle to understand what he was saying and led me to the building he had described.

As soon as I reached it I saw the words 'City Archives' written in German. *This is cool*, I thought. My study of my family's genealogy had increased, particularly my German side. Inside this building I encountered a very sweet, young, bookish sort of a woman who obviously ran the place. I managed to tell her about my family who had lived in the city around the turn of the century. She disappeared for a few minutes after telling me to wait.

The archivist returned with a very old book, which looked like some sort of ledger. She opened to a page and laid the book in front of me. I must have literally gasped and said something like, "Oh shit!" In front of me were the original records of my grandmother's entire family with names, dates, places of birth, marriages and…the signature of my great-grandfather. To an amateur genealogist like myself, this was like hitting a gold mine. The archivist very graciously made copies of the pages for me.

As I was walking back to the hotel, basking in the glory of my find, it suddenly occurred to me – *My God, that was way too weird...a gift from my grandmother!*

I walked into another shop located on a cobblestone side street in town. This particular shop caught my attention because it sold various German antiquities. Inside I browsed around looking at the diverse odds and ends, mostly from the First World War. The shopkeeper was a very pleasant woman with an engaging friendly smile who spoke a bit of English.

Same as I did with the bookstore proprietor, I chatted with the woman about my visiting the hometown of my grandmother. I also mentioned my grandmother's father, my great-grandfather, had been a photographer. She recognized the name and pulled out an old picture, a "cart-de-visite" from the shelf and showed me the back of the photo. Sure enough, there was the logo my great-grandfather used on all his photographs. I didn't think much else of the coincidence and actually must have gotten distracted when other customers walked into the shop. I left the shop content enough with the coincidence of seeing one of my great-grandfather's products.

That night in bed, I lay awake and thought, *I need to go back to that shop and see that photograph again.* I am not sure why I had this thought, but it was a nagging task I knew I needed to do. I did not have a lot of time to complete this because I only had a few hours to see the rest of the town and get back to Frankfurt in time for the flight to my next destination. I had allotted only two days in my grandmother's town.

In actuality, I had practically no time. It turned out the shops opened later on weekends, and I really needed to get on the road back to Frankfurt. I was waiting at the front door as the shop opened. I was obsessed with seeing that photograph again. I figured I would buy it since it was one of my great-grandfather's pieces. Again the shopkeeper was as friendly as could be. I asked her if I could see the photograph she had shown me the previous day and she took it off the shelf and handed it to me. I looked at the photograph and was immediately stunned. Staring out at me from the picture were the faces of two of my grandmother's sisters, my great-aunts when they were children!

I was excited and asked the shopkeeper if I could purchase the photograph. She said very softly, "I am very sorry, but the picture is not for sale." I must have looked crestfallen, because in the next instant she said, "but for you, Sir, it is a gift." Grandma had done it! In the two days I spent in her hometown, I received two gifts.

I have learned many things in my readings and received much guidance from a friend (Mark) and my family members. They have helped me unravel family secrets, but they NEVER told me anything flat out. I had to learn and figure things out myself, with only a little clue here and there. By doing this, they have taught me one very important thing. They will not lead our lives—we are meant to live our own lives.

William's guides provided him with a foundation of knowledge, but would never tell him how to use it. In our sessions, I admired his ability to accept small golden nuggets of information and be satisfied with what was given to him.

He never pressured spirit for more. William said he always knew his messages would become clearer when they needed. Often spirit will deliver parts of messages and not reveal all the information they know to the sitter, insuring they do not interfere with the sitter's life lessons.

Families give us an opportunity to travel closely with other souls. We all have our unique family members and no doubt there are days we love them and days we think we can do without them. Understand it is all done in the interest of learning and refining our relationships.

The next experience I want to share is about an incredible close family, who happen to be my neighbors. I was asked to come over and help out with my friend Moose. I ended up visiting him twice a day until his passing, offering whatever services I could to help out.

Moose was paralyzed from the neck down and had not been eating. When he did eat he could not keep it down. His parents had called me over before to their house to give him massage and Reiki. They were concerned and devastated about his well being. Moose could not talk to his parents to let them know if he was all right, at least talk to them in the traditional sense. Moose was a fifteen-year-old chocolate lab. The question that was being proposed that day was if his parents should assist him in his passing.

On a Friday I walked across the street through their front door; Moose was straining his neck around to look me in the eyes. I sat on the floor around the puppy pads beneath him. When I touched Moose he conveyed his wishes to me. Moose did not straight out talk to me in words per say but his messages were clear. He telepathically told me he was going to get better on Sunday that he was going to walk. The outcome seemed bleak but he made it clear there was to be no assisting. Moose informed me he was not going to leave until he knew for certain his daddy was going to be happy.

Sunday came and went. Moose's parents told me he tried

with all his might that day to get up and walk. In the night his condition worsened. He told me his daddy talked to him about leaving, that it was ok to let go, but he did not believe him. Moose again said he did not want to be assisted. After some persistence I asked if he could pretend if he were too sick to talk to me and he needed to be assisted? "How would you want it done?"

Moose's next message was, "By Thursday at 4pm, if I am not better, my daddy can decide to assist me." He stated his wishes to go at home with his parents beside him, or else he would not do it. I heard he always did what he wanted, including jumping over six foot fences and taking swims in strangers' back yard pools.

Moose was so adored by his daddy's family; they drove each day into Atlanta to help take care of him. Each day I walked across the street to see how he was doing and to relay any messages. Just like any one who is challenged by the process of death, you change your mind and your feelings during the ups and downs. I did my best to keep a close tab on how he felt.

Moose's parents invited me over for dinner on Wednesday night. As I sat down to a wonderfully home cooked meal I made it clear that after dinner I would talk to any spirits who were there to help Moose. He was lying on the floor in a position where he could watch us eat. It made him feel like his was begging, an old favorite pastime of his.

Halfway through dinner his spirit guides began chatting my ear off. (Sometimes you just have to give in.) Moose's daddy's grandmother came through and pleaded with her grandson to let Moose come home. She also announced she would be Moose's new owner and told of how she will let him play with his family. "He's ready to come home now, let him come to me. I will take very good care of him."

Thursday came. The vet showed up at the house at 5:30pm. I called up and asked to come over. As I walked across the street I knew this would be the last time I would physically see Moose. I knew he was ready. I came through the front door without knocking. The family and veterinarian were laid out around Moose almost mimicking the baby Jesus in the manger. Everyone was full of emotion; the vet was calm. Spirit lined up behind Moose and he whispered to me, "I am ready to go."

Moose's daddy reluctantly did the most unselfish act a father could ever do and authorized the vet to assist Moose so he could be free. He lay over Moose with his mouth next to his ear coaching him on. Listening to Moose's daddy whisper words of encouragement and hearing Moose's last words, "Thank you daddy, thank you daddy, thank you daddy," I was a ball of tears. Here I am, the neighbor, allowed to come in at such an intimate moment to witness how much love there can be between a dog and his family. Moose was clearly their only son and now he was dying.

When he left his body there was great rejoice in the room among all the spirits. I was strained between enormous amounts of grief and happiness. All I could do was smile. Moose was happy.

The spirit guides gathered around Moose's new form, petting him, squeezing him, cooing. I have never witnessed a reunion before. I was so lucky to be there for his. I still sometimes find it strange I have such sadness related to death, when in reality it is a rite of passage, a wondrous celebration of freedom.

I told Moose he can come across the street and see me anytime. I have seen him on a few occasions always full of life. I include my pets as children and even go as far as writing about them in my annual Holiday letter. I know their souls are in my life for some destined reason. Animals give unconditionally; it is all they know, much like a parent child relationship instead of an owner pet one.

At this stage in my journey I cannot imagine life without

my parents and I hope they stay on this side with me for many years to come. I love my parents- all four of them. When I work with people who live without one or more of their parents my heart goes out to them. I hope they each find a way to connect which helps fill any void they have.

One session comes to mind where a father came through for his daughter. He took his time and explained to his "little girl" about love. She was having difficulty choosing between two people she loved dearly; one was a man and the other a woman. She could have a lifestyle that would fit into society and not be bothered about the difficulties of being in a same sex relationship. Her father explained each person's pros and cons and how each love is reflected in her life. He clearly told his daughter the love she shared with the woman was far more pure and rewarding to her than the man.

After his reassurance about her commitment to love, he pulled a young woman in spirit close to him and began to introduce her to his daughter as his granddaughter.

The young woman opened with, "Mom, I am your daughter."

I interrupted and told her she looked about 24 years old.

"I took the name you wanted to use. You know, the family name, it is biblical but not too biblical. My name is Ruth; Ruthie is what I go by."

She replied, "I don't have any children."

I asked the sitter over the phone if she had a daughter or a miscarriage about 24 years ago. There was silence for some time.

"I did have one miscarriage...in the late 70s. I can't believe this. Ruth is my Grandmother's name. I love that name."

The father explained how Ruthie did not want to reincarnate to any one else and chose to stay with him. He ended with how wonderful a mother she has been to many other people. There was no need to question her ability to be a woman, but she needed to question what love would be best for her and allow herself to experience it.

Each time I facilitate a parent/child reconnection, the bond I have with each of my parents is strengthened. Even after parents pass on the relationship can still grow. Below Randee shares her unbelievable journey of how spirit helped her understand her father's passing before it occurred and how the reunion of both her parents assists her in life. Her accounts took place over several phone readings.

When Life Serves You Up Lemons
Randee, 44, Hypnotherapist, Boca Raton, Florida

I remember my brother Adam telling me a very dear, mutual friend had been to Jamie in January 2001 for a reading, during which she communicated with our mother. She gave details about my father, Norman, who at the time was terminally ill with cancer.

Norman was diagnosed in December 2000 and passed in February 2001. No one would have guessed his illness would progress so quickly. The message relayed from my mother to Adam was "on his next visit to Florida he should tell his father goodbye because he [my father] would be departing soon after this." In addition, my mother conveyed her excitement for their reunion and how she was planning a big party decorated with balloons for his return. Subsequently, my brother came to Florida and did not leave until our father passed on February 8th, 2001.

Several days before Dad passed, he appeared to fall asleep. When he opened his eyes he told me about his visit to Norman's party. He told me about all the beautiful colors of the balloons and what a wonderful party it was. (I had not shared this information with him.) We talked about the party up until his passing, which gave him something positive to focus on.

Once Dad passed I had a strong desire to communicate with him and I sensed Jamie would be the one to connect us. It was nearly two months after his passing when I had my first appointment. From the moment I said hello it was as if someone turned on a faucet, tears poured from my eyes.

First thing, Jamie told me my father was right there in the room with her. I cannot express in words the emotions stirred inside of me. After accurately describing him, Jamie passed along his opening message, which was to thank me for taking care of him and how much it meant to have me with him through his illness. Then he said, "You were right; there was a party waiting for me when I crossed over into the light."

Many confirming details have been conveyed through Jamie. My father reminded me, "That was quite a stunt I pulled, wasn't it?"

"Daddy what are you talking about?"

"Remember when I said to everybody 'Not yet?'"

At that moment I knew 100%, without any doubt whatsoever, I was communicating with my father. Four days before he passed there were about fifty people in his room, he told everybody he was going to be leaving and hugged and kissed every person in the room, which brought tears to everyone over the sadness of losing him. He closed his eyes leaving us to believe he was gone. A few minutes later he opened up his eyes and said "Not yet".

The room was heavy with emotion at this incredibly intense moment. Everyone had been so hysterical crying that we turned to laughter at his remark. Unless a person was in his bedroom that day, which Jamie was not, they would have never known this happened.

When Jamie is communicating my father to me, it is in his vocabulary; he was very articulate and chose his words carefully. She also fittingly depicts his hand gestures. He always communicated with his hands when he spoke in a way unique to him.

Connecting through Jamie is like having my mother and father on the other end of the phone. I hear her voice, but I visualize them. When I speak with my mother her humor comes through, her sense of jubilation, and the intense love she exuded. As Jamie describes her, she captures my mom's bright effervescent smile, hair-dos, clothes, and body structure.

My mother passed twenty-five years prior and it was beautiful when Dad declared they were finally together. In fact, right after Dad passed I walked outside to gather myself and reflect. I looked skyward and saw a shooting star complimented by a giant harvest moon. What timing it was for me to witness a star flying across the night's sky!

My father recounted this moment saying, "Remember

when you went outside and you saw the shooting star in the sky? That was your Mother and I dancing." They were eloquent dancers. From the time I was a little girl I loved watching them. It is one of the things I remember most about them. They danced as if they were floating on clouds and I knew this was a sign to let me know they were reunited.

My mother died of a heart attack in our home in New Jersey. On that day my brother Adam, who was ten years old at the time, was in the house alone with her. Our neighbor Naomi happened to come over moments before my mother fell back onto the bed, dying instantly. Naomi was there for Adam. This is information no one would know or could pull out of a hat.

I mention this because on the day my father died, about a half hour prior to his passing, Naomi arrived in Florida. (I had been in contact with her to tell her my Dad was ill and dying.) That evening I got a phone call telling me she was at the airport. Adam had not seen her since my mother's passing. I gave Naomi directions and she literally walked into my father's bedroom as he took his last breath. It was Naomi, Adam, and myself in his room as he departed. It was absolutely incredible for her to arrive at that moment.

While talking with Jamie I was told, "Oh it was no accident that Naomi was in the room." Jamie knew Naomi's name and everything. I inquired to the purpose of her being there and then my mother came through and said Naomi is an Earth Angel and she was sent to help us with our father's passing. Jamie amazed me talking about Naomi.

My father's way of dealing with certain issues is still the same. He offers advice telling me "to be cautious" and "take the safe route." My mother continues to have the same strong, loving hand balanced with a lot of emotion and kindness. She talks to me about my children, mothering, and brings up things from when I was a child. Sometimes their words are firm, almost harsh, in the sense of "don't do that" or "do this" and what I have realized is their positioning as parents isn't different despite their spirit state.

Dad also thanked me for handling the arrangements for his burial at sea; he is "grateful it was so beautiful that day and he really appreciated all the arrangements you made." Jamie described the entire day as she expressed Dad's gratitude. She even narrated the words from my father's eulogy, "One of the life lessons that my Dad taught me was when life serves you up lemons, not only should you make lemonade, but you should share it with everyone you love and as I look around the room I see he obviously quenched a lot of thirst."

On July 4, 2003 my brothers and I had a session with Jamie in person. Jamie sat on the floor in front of us. She took a deep breath and her body leaned forward as her head fell gently towards her lap. When she raised her head, she looked intensely at each of us and began by saying "It has been such a long time since I've had all of my children together."

What happened next floored both Gary and me. Adam did not catch this because he was too young when Mom passed to remember. After wiping her eyes, she took the tissue and twirled it until the entire tissue was twisted. Then she unraveled it, placed it on her thigh, smoothed it out, and proceeded to fold the tissue again and again until it was in a neat, tiny, perfect little square! This unique habit was something my mother did frequently in life. As she spoke to us she touched her eyebrow and played with Jamie's hair. Anyone who knew my mom well could confirm she did this ALL THE TIME!

I never doubted I communicated with my parents when I had sessions on the phone with Jamie, but I must confess the intensity of actually SEEING my mother's gestures, ones that I have not witnessed in over 25 years, was further confirmation for me that our souls live on!

Jamie's extraordinary gift bridges the gap between this world and that of those who have passed. I am eternally grateful to her for easing my pain and filling my heart and soul with inner peace.

Through my experiences with Jamie I have been blessed with a sense of security, knowing that one-day I too shall pass into the light and be reunited with my loved ones!

From the start it was easy to talk with Randee's parents. Their presence is undeniable and strong. Usually hours before the reading these two like to contact me to let me know they will be there. Twice they woke me in the morning to let me know of their impending afternoon arrival. It is their way of leaving a message with me and one I do not recommend other spirit beings following.

Often the sitter's spirit guides come see me right before the appointment time, but on the occasion before Thomas came to my house, no one showed up. I wondered if he was going to make it. Frequently when the sitter can't come, either spirit will not show up or they will come tell me personally that the sitter will not make it. This time; however, Thomas showed up at our scheduled time. I opened the door to see his aura shining like a beacon of light. It was a surprise and a beautiful sight. I hugged him before introducing myself and asked him, "Why are you here?"

I told him he has what I have, (which made it sound like some common cold) and I could not help him. There is a first time for everything, but at that moment I just knew I was not giving this man a reading. I invited him back to the office anyway, since he was insisting someone had to be there for him. As soon as I got comfortable on the floor I felt like I was about to fall into a deep sleep, which is the feeling I get when I channel. I quickly explained to Thomas what was about to happen, who was in the room with us, and managed to say, "You were right," before I left my body.

Who Asked Your Pot to Boil?
Thomas, Ageless, Singer, Atlanta, GA

One of my dear friends recommended I see a spiritual consultant he had seen several times. At the time, I was having difficulties with my voice. I had a polyp on my vocal cord and wanted to avoid surgery. My voice was very hoarse and I became concerned for my singing career. I worked as a marketing manager for an industrial distribution company; however, I planned to leave that job for my singing and entertainment career. I also desired to incorporate spiritual teaching into my songs and speaking engagements; making my voice EXTREMELY important to me.

I made an appointment with Jamie and the night before it I could not sleep. I was disturbed all night. I had a very vivid dream about being in high school and going to my first day of classes. It was my senior year and I couldn't find my homeroom class. I remember looking in several rooms attached to a long hallway, and each time I walked to a door—it shut. It was as if I was going to the wrong doors. Finally the correct one was opening and I awoke as I walked through this doorway.

I knew when I went to see Jamie, I would experience meeting the spirit of a person I had never physically met, but who has always been a part of my life. As I got to Jamie's door, I could tell something wonderful was going to happen. After opening the door she gave me a hug and said, "Why are you here?" She explained, "You have what I have, I don't know what I can do for you." I informed Jamie that I knew there was someone who I thought wanted to talk with me and I felt they would be present.

Jamie took me from her living room into her office. She explained how normally spirits or energies that want to come through will make an appearance to her before the client gets to her house for the consultation. However, my spirits or angels didn't show up beforehand, and she thought this was an indication I might not show either. As I entered her treatment room, they appeared. She told me who some of the spirits were. She described my father, whom I have never physically met, perfectly. (I did not tell Jamie beforehand that my father was deceased or how he died.) I knew he would be the one spirit to come through for sure.

He was on my right side along with other spirits from his side of the family; I think my grandfather and an uncle were present. On my left side were my grandmother (Gertrude), and possibly my aunt Anna (or Nan as we called her), as well as some other spirits. Jamie called my grandmother "Gerdie," which may have been a nickname for her during her life. Jamie said Gerdie didn't want to say anything; she wanted to be next to me. I remember my Grandmother before she died when I was about four years old. My mother told me she had blessed me as a child to do great things to share with the world.

Jamie sat on the floor while I opted to sit on the sofa. She said she was going to channel because my father strongly wanted to come through. For a moment Jamie didn't think she would be able to do the channeling, and what transpired was more than interesting. My father was very pushy and forceful. I was a bit nervous because I knew I was going to meet my father for the first time. Strangely, I felt at peace also. I was eager to meet and talk to him.

After closing her eyes, Jamie took a couple of deep breaths and her head slumped, then she slowly raised her head with closed eyes. Her facial expression changed and I must say she looked like my father. I knew his energy was present from the way he spoke and his appearance in Jamie's body.

My father reached for me without speaking a word. He was crying, holding me and rubbing my hands. I began crying like a baby. He started by saying, "I'm sorry! I'm so sorry for leaving you! I'm sorry! I'm so sorry!" Over and over again, my father apologized for dying and leaving me when I was six months old. I reassured him it was okay. I was fine and I loved him. He said "you were so young, just a baby. I know you are fine because your mother did a great job with you, but I should have been there and I'm sorry." He acknowledged that I have my mother's hands, which I do. He also said that he was impressed with the way I had taken care of myself in life physically, mentally, financially, and most of all spiritually.

I sat on the floor with my father listening to him tell me how proud he was of the things I have done; he was present at my high school and college graduations. He was especially pleased when I walked across the stage to receive my college degree. He told me he has always been with me and that I have become more aware of this as I get older. He expressed how excited he was when "they" told him he would see me today. He knew he would talk with me, but he did not know he would have the opportunity to hold me. His excitement provoked him to keep me up "all last night." He apologized for that, but he could not help himself. He told me he caused me to dream about my first day as a senior in high school. My actual senior year was incredible; I was tops in my class and involved in everything imaginable. It was a time in my life I could relate to going though a door in life. My graduation speech was entitled "The Opening of a New Door." I guess this was fitting for how my life would change after meeting my father and Jamie.

My father and I talked about my mother and how she has a special place in the universe for the great job she has done rearing my three older sisters and me. He told me about meeting my mother when they were both teachers and how he had to go through the entire family, especially the girls (my three older sisters), to get to finally marry her. My mother had been married before, and gave birth to my sisters. Her first husband died, and some years later she met my father and they eventually married. He shared a story about my sisters giving him a hard time and wanting to throw him in the boiling pot.

I wasn't aware of this story so afterwards I asked my mother to tell me about my sisters' reaction to my father wanting to marry her. The first thing she told me was about Muriel, my sister, and the boiling pot. The story behind this is my father told my sisters that he was going to marry my mother. Muriel said, "No you're not!" My father responded, "Who asked your pot to boil? (Meaning who asked you anything?)" Muriel said, "I'll show you a boiling pot. Come on Anna, let's boil him." They grabbed my father by the arms and tried to pull him in the kitchen to put him in a pot and boil him. They were kidding of course and ended up laughing and wrestling with him for fun. How interesting to have that confirmed!

My father explained how when he died he made a special agreement with God to bless and watch over me. He let me know the hand of God is with me in life and that I have always been special. He said I knew something was different about me all my life, but I didn't quite know what it was. According to him this was because I have been given special gifts and talents, and he is proud of me for realizing these gifts and for my desire to share them with the world.

I have always known one day I will write a book about my life experiences. My father said he has seen the book I am going to write. He believes I am very talented and advised me to never worry about what other people have to say regarding my abilities and cautioned me to never compare myself to others and by following this advice, I will be extremely successful in life.

I could barely talk during this entire experience, but it didn't matter. Looking back, I recall my voice being clear as I spoke to him. I don't remember having any problems at all during the two hours. Only afterwards did I remember having problems with my voice.

My father said it was time to leave my job of ten years. I needed to grow and become part of the world. I have many things to do and I was at the point where my happiness would no longer come from working in the corporate arena. He explained I "have to share what God has given me with the world." He said he would always be with me. He would communicate to me more often and help open doors when I thought they could not be opened – just like in my dream the previous night. It excited him so much to see and actually touch me he stated, "I think I'm going to have another heart attack." That blew me away since my father died from alcoholism and had a heart attack. Jamie had no knowledge of this.

I expressed my forgiveness to my father for him not being alive during my life. It was also important for me to let him know I love him and to know he loves me as well. He started crying again at this point and said he wanted to give me a gift. He placed his hand over my throat and held it there for a while. I started to cry as I felt the energy rush through my body. He closed with, "I must go now, they are telling me I have to go." He gave me a very tight hug and simply slipped away.

Two hours had passed as Jamie came back and told me what she experienced. She said she didn't remember anything, but she felt as if she were hovering above the room watching a man wearing a blue sweater and glasses holding a baby in his arms as he paced the floor talking to the child. What is amazing about this description is the only existing picture of my father and me is from when I was five months old. He is holding me in his arms and in the photograph he is wearing a blue sweater and glasses. Jamie knew nothing of this photo.

Jamie and I talked for 20 or 30 minutes about what happened and how I felt. I was pleased and emotionally drained at the same time. I was excited about talking with my father for the first time in this life. I knew it would happen long before I got to Jamie's that day. Now I feel the presence of my father all the time and I talk with him frequently. When I need him, he is always here for me and I am proud that I've learned more about my own gifts to communicate spiritually. It enables me to keep peace within myself no matter what I'm facing. I will never forget my experience with Jamie because it was truly as if I walked through a new and glorious open door with my life.

When I returned to my body two hours later, my inner clock felt like five minutes had passed. I was thinking it was too soon for me to come back because I heard Thomas weeping. My body felt completely empowered and whole when I opened wet eyes to the sight of Thomas sitting directly in front of me. He explained how his father's crying made my face wet. The strange thing was I did not feel any repercussions of crying since I wasn't emotionally involved. I am humbled and so grateful to be a part of Thomas' connection with his father. Spirit knew what they were doing when they ignored me that day. By withholding their input at the beginning, I experienced the profoundness of this reunion at a deeper level.

Two months after this appointment, Thomas had surgery. We spoke briefly over the phone about his procedure and the associated risks. Thomas divulged how frightened he was because his voice is his livelihood. His father responded with last minute reassurance that everything was going to be okay. Thomas was pleased to hear his doctor's words following the surgery, "You are the poster child for God's perfect vocal chords."

I often watch as others are reunited with their family but on rare occasions I find myself in their shoes. My father explains how our family members who have passed on still participate in our family.

"Hiroshima?"

Joel, 59, Tree Farmer: Butler Tree Farm, Inventor of: Cool Ring, father of Jamie, Lakeland, FL

My family and I were in upper state New York, Syracuse, for a family reunion with my wife's family. It was our last day before we all fly back to our homes. We were all visiting the old historic farming museum. While we were in the wood working room of the museum Jamie comes up to me and asks, "Guess who is here?" I know when Jamie gets this gleam in her speech she is hinting this person is in spirit. The obvious answer would be her Grandfather Jones. He is her mother's father that worked with wood. He and Jamie always had a special bond. Granddad Jones looks out for Jamie. Jamie went on to translate Granddad's advice. He was telling me about my tractor back at the farm in Florida. He advised me to order special motor oil and not to change the oil too often; the tractor needed it to run through the engine to work out the motor. Then he went on to tell me about some tractor repairs that need to be made. I have not told Jamie before that I order special tractor oil from Texas and which tractor needs what kind of repair. Theses are topics we do not discuss when we get together. By now the rest of the family has caught up with us. Granddad Jones went on to tell Jason, my son, about the flight back to Atlanta. Jason has a strong fear of flying. If it wasn't for the love of his wife Lucy he would never get on a plane. He told Jason that the flight would be smooth with very little turbulence, a very graceful take off, yet when it comes time to landing that we will not land on time. There will be no problems with the plane or terrorists, but you will have to stay in the air. Fortunately for Jason we were on the same flight to Atlanta before we split up to our destinations. As we were nearing Atlanta what seemed for no reason the plane performed a hard right turn. Many of the passengers were alarmed by the sudden change. This sent Jason off the charts, even the drinks he had consumed were not calming his nerves. A few moments later the pilot comes over the pa and announces that Atlanta Airport is experiencing a back up due to the amount of air traffic and we will be delayed for landing until we are cleared. We all remember what Granddad had said earlier and this somewhat sooth Jason's flying panic; at least he had no room to doubt that was the real cause for the delay. Usually he would have created a complete scenario in his head out of fear.

I always enjoy listening to Jamie give messages from my Granddad Freeman. One time he mentioned to me "How do you like you cottage at Rhey, NH.

"Hiroshima?" I used to vacation at his home is Rhey when I was a boy. He had a flagpole stuck in a mound in the ground on the side yard. He was always collection an item here and there. He called his home sweet home Hiroshima because he felt it looked like a bomb got dropped on it. That was fascinating to hear Jamie tell details of our family that was long before her time.

Chapter
— NINE —

Taking Care of Business

"The only tyrant I accept in this world is the 'still small voice' within me."
—Mahatma Gandhi (1869-1948)

Business can be a confusing, frustrating, and rewarding venture. Many sitters inquire about the steps they should take to ensure their success. The most amusing session I've had was with a businessman in 1999. He came into the office with a Rolex shining under the sleeve of his white linen Ralph Lauren shirt. The only detail I knew prior to our meeting was his name; I was clueless as to how he acquired his money. His personality was abrasive and narrow as he told me he did not "believe in any of this psychic shit." The only reason he came to see me was because he knew two people who raved about their experiences with me and he wanted to try me out for himself.

As soon as I started the reading I heard from his spirit guide. "He is scamming his employees. He is milking them. He has to stop because he is about to get caught. This is serious." *I thought, maybe I'm not hearing this correctly* and again the words repeated. *O.K. I'll tell him.*

As soon as I passed along this warning with more details that came through, he stood, said thank you, and dropped a C-note on the floor. He was in and out of my office less than ten minutes. I watched him as he left, walked up the sidewalk, and got into his car. Evidently I was told more than he was willing or wanting revealed to me. I thought he was going to pass out from the experience.

Other sessions based on business have been phenomenal. Details from fundraising and accounting to employee personality conflicts clearly channel through. Because spirit uses jargon specific to the sitter's area of interest it may sound like I have a business degree, which is far from my reality. Nevertheless, I enjoy these readings tremendously because the topic of discussion is outside my general knowledge.

Before I met the next sitter, I had an intensely strange dream relating to a spa/massage business. Dreams, for me, are the subconscious' way of feeding the conscious mind information. It was so real I remembered all the details, from architecture to colour, several weeks after having the dream. In the subconscious scenario I was leaving my gym, still dressed in athletic clothes, and instead of returning home I walked past Piedmont Park and went into a spa.

The entrance was spectacular: two stories of glass glowing in a blue hue with the sound of a trickling brook in the background. The design was simple, clean and blue; a blue glow reminiscent of fresh tropical ocean water, without a hint of turquoise. There was a crescent shaped reception desk, circular chairs in the waiting area, and a floor as smooth and white as newly polished marble. I glimpsed a shop vending aromas for the mind, body, and soul. A staircase lead upward to the treatment rooms where one could receive various modalities of bodywork. It was a wonderful peaceful space. I awoke feeling refreshed and calm, wishing there was such a place. I understood this dream weeks later when John came in for a reading.

The Blue Med Spa
John, 32, Medical Supply Sales Rep, Miami Native

I didn't have reservations about going to Jamie since my partner had already experienced a very moving and amazing encounter with her. After hearing about his experience I thought, maybe I need to go see her. I've always kept an open mind to these kinds of things, but I didn't know what to expect. I went into my consultation hopeful that I would receive helpful information to assist me with my business venture. Just meeting Jamie was wonderful, my first experience was interesting and I enjoyed her energy.

I took a seat on her antique purple couch, while Jamie sat on the floor. Before we got started I briefly explained to her what I had done with another spa and how it sparked my desire to open one of my own; yet, it was my plan to have a unique offering for the clientele. Jamie stopped me to interject she had a dream about ten days prior where she was leaving her gym near her home in Midtown, and she saw the sign for this place that was like a spa and she went inside.

She drew a picture for me of the reception area. There was a crescent shaped desk and the walls were a pretty blue hue. She also illustrated for me some little round chairs. What she drew was very similar to a photo I had from a magazine. I saved it because I liked the layout. She continued telling me how she observed a room where there would be an aromatherapist of sorts. It would be like going to the pharmacist; an apothecary where the person mixes things for specific conditions. The overall space was lofty. Jamie shared with me the vision I was having of what is to be Blue

Med Spa, without knowing more about the business I was planning.

I then told Jamie what I envisioned for a medical spa where people will be able to have medical treatments like plastic surgery, oncololgy, pre- and post-operative treatments, as well as holistic spa experiences. It would provide a combination of wellness and anti-aging services.

During the first session there was an Englishman who came through strongly. He showed up to discuss business. He was described as being a snappy dresser and humorous. He called himself Randy—short for Randall. I had been looking for a location for the spa, which I wanted to be in midtown and checked potential spots, but nothing was ideal.

While talking with Jamie, she drew a picture of 10th street where it intersects Juniper and Peachtree Street. She circled the area of 10th street. I already knew there was nothing there since I scouted this area several times. I thought this was the best place for the business, but nothing was available to lease. This was in August of 2001.

The next time I went to Jamie was right after Thanksgiving, November 2001. Right before this second session Andrew, my real estate broker, called to make me aware of a property that had come available to lease. I was curious about the location and he informed me it was near the intersection of Piedmont and 10th, between Juniper and Piedmont. I was so surprised I asked, "Where?"

Going back to my notes from the first session I confirmed what I remembered Jamie showing me. This was the exact area she circled on the map she had drawn for me. Immediately I wanted to know if we could look at this building, but I had an appointment with Jamie set before I had a chance to see this property.

This time Randy channeled through Jamie, who was wearing Gap overalls. He observed the clothing on the body he was using and said, "I would never be caught dead wearing something like this." Now that's funny considering...

Randy told me about the broker of the vacant space. He explained it was someone I had spoken with before, but I was sure I had not seeing how I haven't called on any other real estate brokers. He described this man as a "pat me on the back kind of guy." Randy told me to ask the realtor what he knows about the area and what he's done. "He will fill your ear with all kinds of things and this will make him feel good about himself. The realtor will want you to have the property."

That night I called Andrew to ask whom we were meeting the next day. He gave me the other broker's name and I shouted, "No way! That guy?"

When I was looking at other locations someone referred me to this man. I had actually spoken with this broker two or three times, eight months prior. The description I had gotten from Randy was completely true for this guy. The realtor knew everything—all the details of Midtown. Having this insight helped me communicate with the broker better and reminded me to ask specific questions.

The Englishman also gave me ideas about how to bring financing to the project, providing me options. I had not considered using multi-media venues and Randy directed me to a graphic designer who created a multi media marketing presentation to present Blue Med Spa to investors. In our final session together, Randy acknowledged I had followed his advice without my explaining to Jamie what actions I had taken.

These events have been great guidance for me. Subsequently, I have been able to structure a deal to purchase the building instead of leasing it. It is so wild for me to review my interactions with Jamie: the description from her dream, the pinpoint of the location, the connection with this broker and all the market advice. Everything has worked out well. Because I received information supportive of my desires, I know that I am assisted from beyond to manifest this business.

John has created an incredible sensation of the fountain of youth with his Blue Med Spa. The dream and the sessions guided him further into a venture that initially was too overwhelming.

The following story reflects the need for reminders as well as guidance. Sometimes we forget what we have been told and frequently ask for advice without following through on it. This is where Sheri found herself.

Sheri is a type of woman who has so much energy inside of her, even when she whispers; her sound travels the length of a football field. When you walk away from her you are charged up for the rest of the day. Even though this beaming woman has so much she needed to focus on conquering her fear of success. Through out her sessions she battled with the advice her guides provided, not because it fell on deaf ears, but because it sounded too far-fetched. By taking risks and putting faith in her guides' words, Sheri has grown with confidence. To her determination I recite a quote from a famous marketing advertisement of the 80's: "You've come a long way baby."

Queen of Fear
Sheri, 35, Healer/Writer, Atlanta, GA

On March 10, 1999 my maternal grandmother died in Detroit. I had a poor relationship with her and didn't know how to feel when she passed. I left graduate school in Atlanta, Georgia and flew home to attend the funeral. It was a stressful experience that sent me back to psychotherapy sessions. Upon returning to Atlanta, my boyfriend called to tell me James Van Praagh was scheduled to be in town on March 18 at a local bookstore. I knew I had to go get my book signed and see if I could find out anything about my recently deceased grandmother.

I got there about 30 minutes before he was to appear and joined the lengthy line. When Van Praagh arrived, the bookstore representative informed us the author had already been to three other bookstores and would only be signing books. We would not be allowed to talk with him, which disappointed me. When my turn came, I noticed he looked exhausted, but his piercing blue eyes had a gentle presence. I gave him the books I intended to send to my grieving mother and her two sisters.

James Van Praagh looked up at me from his table and asked, "Are you aware you are a healer?"

"You think so?" I sputtered.

"I know so."

I persisted, "How do you know?"

"I can see the pretty green in your aura."

"Strange…you know you're the second medium in the last month to tell me this." I said. (The first one was in Boston)

"Do you need a third? I see you working in a hospital later on. What is it you do for a living?"

"I'm pursuing a doctorate in literature. Well, what do you mean by 'healer'? I can't cure cancer and I don't have a medical background, I promise you."

He says, "This is what I see. Teaching is a form of healing, you know."

"Well, what am I supposed to do with this healing ability?"

"Read my books for starters in order to begin to develop your healing abilities and go from there. Also, begin meditating."

I thanked him. I stifled the desire to touch him, but then he'd already touched me with the message he chose to impart. Feeling pressured by the bookstore representative's anxious glare, I stepped away from the table and situated myself about 3 feet away. I wanted to hear what he had to say to others. After all, he could have been saying the same thing to everyone to sell more books. I stayed for about 30 minutes, but I didn't overhear anything similar. Just small talk about mutual acquaintances, website and the like. Finally, I drove home in a haze.

I needed greater spiritual insight into what was happening in my life and the kind of answers I needed couldn't be supplied in 30 to 40 minute tarot card or psychometry readings. During the fall of 1999, I'd seen a pleasant looking, young blond woman on a local Atlanta morning show that was reading people's auras. I scribbled her phone number on a yellow sticky note, but didn't call immediately. As a matter of fact, the piece of paper languished on the back of my dusty nightstand for about 4 months. In late January, I was at the end of my rope and hungered for answers, so I called the number.

Jamie Butler answered. I told her how I'd seen her on television and was interested in finding out more about her work. She explained, "I don't consider myself a psychic. I'm a medium. I am like a human telephone. I could not do what I do without the help of my spiritual guides. I only need your first name and prefer you not tell me anything else about yourself. Come and see me and if my work is not helpful to you, you don't have to pay me anything."

Well, I'd never encountered a reader where pay was optional. I went to see her about two days later. On January 25, 2000 I climbed stairs of a two-story walkup in Virginia Highlands with a large, unwieldy portable stereo in my hand. Unfortunately, I didn't have a micro cassette player to record the session and had brought the next best thing. I knocked on her door and a perky blond with gray, lively eyes answered the door.

She invited me in and I took a seat on the couch in the living room. As I drank a glass of ice water, she settled on the floor with paper and colored pencils. She explained she liked to begin her readings by drawing the client's aura and interpreting it. After finishing, she gently informed me we had company. I looked around expecting someone to come out of the bedroom since I hadn't heard anyone at her front door. I couldn't see or hear no one.

Still not quite understanding, I asked, "Where?"

Jamie gestured toward the corner of the living room, not too far from where I was sitting, an empty corner.

She said, "Three spirits have joined us. They say they are related to you on your mother's side."

Normally, I would've jumped out of my seat and got the hell on out of there, but I didn't budge. I felt no fear, which was highly unusual since I'd grown to look upon myself as the Queen of Fear. It seemed like I'd spent most of my life afraid of the Unknown Factor. To the contrary, I was curious and felt a voracious hunger for answers. My analytical side kicked in and I immediately asked them to prove they were related to me on my mother's side.

Jamie responded with intricate family history that made it obvious the three spirits were my maternal grandmother, Josephine, who crossed over 9 months prior, and her two sisters, Aunts Essie and Susie who died in the early 1980s. It was amazing! Jamie was sitting on the floor writing down everything they were telling her to relay to me.

My Aunt Essie said, "It is me, Auntie. I took care of your mother and I've come to take care of you. I loved your mother. Why would I leave the family when they need help? Alright – here is who has come. Your other aunt and your grandmother. The three sisters are here – that is all. I was elected to talk between the three of us since I do have the best speaking voice. I feel I sing better than them too."

Coming from a somewhat dysfunctional family in which I was not immediately knowledgeable about every nook and cranny of family history, I had to later check on the veracity of my aunt's claim that the three of them were singers. My mother confirmed that they had, indeed, been singers in the church choir together. However, the identity of the superior singer remains open to question.

Aunt Essie continued, "We women are here to talk to you about straightening out your life. You have so much love; yet, no direction, so much passion, but no place to put it. First off, your career —"

"My career?"

"Yes, career before men – for now."

She seemed to have read my mind.

They spoke the desires of my heart, which for years remained unarticulated and laid out much of my life plan with details of how to accomplish it. I listened, went into myself and discovered they had a better sense of my life passion than I realized. They outlined my natural skills, the source of my life passion, and explained the greater spiritual purpose behind the new path I was about to begin. I even received details about my love life and the man I would marry. Lastly, they answered questions about our family dysfunction.

I now call them collectively "My Grandmothers." They reiterated my identity as a healer and said I have the power to heal hearts through my hands, my voice and my bubbly personality, which brings people to me. I began the first stage of my healing journey in January 2000. The Ancestors came directly and informed me they were here to help me get my life in order.

Exactly one year later in January 2001, my Ancestors came back to me through a channeling session with Jamie to say my rest period was over and the second leg of my healing journey was about to begin. It was now time to start a non-denominational spiritual website called SpiritualAtlanta.com where people of all faiths could come and dialogue while accessing spiritual articles and the latest information on events in the metro Atlanta area. This site would be an 'e' Community Center. I informed them they had the wrong person since I am not well versed in technology, coming from a Humanities background as I do. They assured me I was born to do this job and that there was no mistake since I was a World-Bridger. They laid out the pathway for getting started and I did it! My website premiered November 2001.

On July 9, 2002 my Grandmothers came again to

inform me it was time to start the third leg of my healing. They told me to go and find The Awakening Body and there I would find kindred spirits who would be very interested in what I am doing as well as help me continue to heal my many layers. I had never heard of the organization, but I got on my computer and looked it up and easily found Lynn, the owner. As it happens, my email arrived two days before she was having a Saturday workshop on helping women to heal spiritually and sexually in her home.

My healing journey that began in January 2000 has been wonderfully challenging. Although a significant part of my healing work has been done with Jamie, I am always mindful of the fact I can and do frequently contact my ancestors, other spiritual guides and angels on my own. The key is always to go within.

Chapter
— TEN —

Surprise Guests

"To the rationally minded the mental processes
of the intuitive appear to work backwards."
—Frances Wickes

Language, word usage, intonation and accents shine through in readings as much as the messages. There have been several times when a spirit guide had an accent or elaborate vocabulary that I couldn't decipher and I was stumped in a session. A sitter named Edward brought an entourage of guides from the Caribbean. His aunt on his mother's side of the family came through to assist him.

His aunt had a cadence of the islands and Edward explained what I translated from her was presented in "that culturally authoritative way that only a black mother of [his] time would or could know." I can vouch for that because I hesitated to pronounce every other word and would laugh because I knew I was pronouncing it wrong. Luckily Edward understood his aunt's dialect.

In Edward's excitement he called out her name and she told him in a strong voice, "Eddie, dis iz what I waz called, but dat iz not my name." Edward confirmed it was her nickname and added she was the only person he knew to call him by his pet name: Eddie.

Edward also added, "To punctuate the session my aunt was on the money with a response to my statement about needing to find my son. Without any prompting she mentioned my son's mother as an ex-wife. I never said to Jamie that my son and daughter have different mothers. She described my son's mother and her motivations so well that I was simply in disbelief. It was like she knew my ex-wife. And, in retrospect, I realized that they [my aunt and ex-wife] had met in real life. That was awesome." Edward was impressed and surprised his aunt was the one to meet with him because "she was not necessarily what you would call spiritual," but in the end he felt his session couldn't have been better.

Along with hearing the unique language of their loved ones, when the sitter gets to hear the perfect recantation of their family members' last dying wish or words or the deceased's favorite song the sitter gets their "proof of purchase." Here are a few of those sessions I recall.

I remember several years back I was speaking to a daughter whom set up an appointment to speak to her mother that had recently passed away. The connection was clear and I was able to describe the mother, her ailments and how she was in a hospital when she died, with her bed pulled up next to the window. The daughter was moved to hear me know the details of her mother's last days so well. Then the mother kept repeating to me, "All I wanted to do was lay down and die." Dragging out the vowel sounds in "all" and "wanted" in a perfect southern accent.

I questioned the mother if she wanted me to tell this to the daughter. "Oh yes! Tell her….aaaall I waaaanted to do was lay down and die." Well after hearing it a few times it became a little funny to me. So I told the daughter in a lighthearted way, imitating her mother (thinking it was funnier this way). Well I ate my words in the next few moments. The daughter began to cry and tell her mother, "I know, I know, I know. I tried but those nurses kept propping you back up!" Then I realized what the mother was saying was literal, not just some metaphor. The daughter began to tell me that her mother had a hard time eating and keeping it down, so the nurses would prop her up to help the digestion. But, all the mother wanted to do was lay flat and rest before she died. When the end came close the daughter and her sister decided to hold vigil and each would take turns staying over night making sure they would lay their mother down after the nurse left the room.

Once when it was the daughter's turn, she had to leave the room to get something to eat. She made sure her mother was comfortable and laying flat. She felt confident enough she would not be gone long and all was well. Upon returning she found her mother had passed away, and she was sitting up. During her short leave a nurse had come in and sat up the mother stuffed the pillows behind her head, for the sake of digestion. The mother's final wish to lay down and die was not granted.

Another session was from a daughter in the mid-west. She had heard of me years ago and had a session but had called recently to have her second session. When she called in, the spirits lined up in the room. There were seven of them ready to talk it up. The grandparents spoke first, then her father. Her father mentioned how he died and that it was very recent.

"A few weeks ago," the daughter replies.

The father tells her, "I wanted to go for a car ride!" I hear a cry, laughter mix on the other end of the line.

"My father told me the day he died he wanted to take a car ride. I kept thinking he did not know what he was talking about."

The father told her he wanted to take a car ride with her,

so he would have her to himself and they could talk in private. They had a family of four and apparently private time was when you were in the car going to and from your destination. This next one is about a grandmother talking to her granddaughter. I was in a small town in GA listening to several families share their stories of how their houses are haunted when one spirit kept talking to me above and over every one else. I thought, man this woman has something to say, I better tell this woman. I asked the woman if she would be open to listening what her guide wanted to say. She looked a little "gun shy" but agreed. So we went into another room for some privacy.

I mentioned to the woman that her grandmother was here for her. She had recently passed over in the last few years. I describe her looks and how she left this world. The granddaughter acknowledged she understood.

The grandmother immediately began to describe an incident that would happen over the summer to make the woman change about how she sees the world. That the incident would be positive but it would make her buy a new car and become more 'green.'' That the car the granddaughter drives is way to big for her.

The granddaughter told me quickly that this was not her grandmother; she would never concern herself with this kind of thing.

When the grandmother heard this, she sat up straight and told me I better repeat everything she is saying.

"Tell her that I sit at the feet of Jesus everyday.''

I glance at the granddaughter sitting in front of me. She seems to be taken back by the comment. She begins to confide in me that her grandmother's last dying wish was to "sit at the feet of Jesus.'' So this must be her grandmother, though her face was a bit confused.

The grandmother continued, "I sit at the feet of Jesus everyday and he teaches me my lessons. He tells me we are his voice and that we need to spread his word. He tells us that the Earth is dying and we need to take care of it so civilizations will be able to thrive. We need to care for the Earth first instead of being selfish."

The granddaughter looks at me a bit in disbelief and says, "If my grandmother believes in this I guess there is something to it." Though this statement was not convincing, I could see the granddaughter giving her message a lot of thought.

I made sure to head outside and see the guests off. I wanted to see what kind of car this little woman drove. Yep, there it was, a huge extended Yukon.

The last one I will share is from a session I had not too long ago. A woman came into the office as a referral. She was cautious not to give me any details about why she was here, but it was soon apparent. Her fourteen year young son whom had died a few weeks before was ready to talk to his mom. I could describe him easily and shared about his death (from a rare illness). Even though this information was detailed and accurate it wasn't until the mother asked one particular question that turned everybody upside down including myself.

"What did we call the nurses?" the mother politely asked.

"F***kers." said the calm and cute son.

I looked at the mother and shook my head, desperately trying to figure out how I was going to get around this one. The expression on my face must have said it all. The mother encouraged me, "...go on and say it."

I told her it began with an "F" and ended in "E-R-S"

"F***kers!!!" she yells out loudly. "Oh my God, F***kers!! That is right, we called the nurses F***kers!! That's right."

My eyes are saucers by now. I know my business neighbors can hear her yell this out clearly. She then could explain that the nurses who cared for him all mentioned he would not live and to give her son strength they decided to nickname the nurses. This has no reflection of the nurses' care and their hard work they provided. But this one word, one word, allowed this mother to believe her son had lived beyond his illness and became well.

Surprises are fun but surprise spirit guests are eye opening. They are a terrific addition to the ever-steady flow of grandmothers. The next two sitters, Jerry and then Mark, experienced reunions with long lost friends. Unfortunately for Jerry his friend retained his teasing personality.

Oh Judy, Get Over It!
Jerry, 42, Life and Fitness Coach, Atlanta, GA

When I first met Jamie, she knew nothing about me. I went to my first reading quite nervous, since this was new for me. In the back of my mind I was hearing what other people would think about it, all the judgmental comments they would make, but I knew I wanted to experience this to learn more about myself.

My reading was more than general stuff; it was downright specific and on target. My grandmother spoke to me in detail about my relationship with my partner and even talked about his poor eating habits. (The truth is they can be bad.) She mentioned when he comes home from work, he will go through a whole bag of potato chips and called him a "chip-a-holic". Also she said he could spend his money better, noting his willingness to spend excessively for a t-shirt. Both of these small details are very true of him. (I can't keep a bag of chips in the house.)

She added, "He has *everything* in his life in its place, in perfect order, but he can not do that with his heart. Your

tenderness fills a void created in his formative years."
She commented on how he likes to be pampered and
to approach him in this way when I make suggestions.
"Don't teach, pamper," she said. This new approach
takes practice but does create an easier environment
for us both.

Another spirit channeled through Jamie and his
opening remark revealed his sense of humor. This
spirit was my old roommate, Steve, from Chicago. He
caught me off-guard when he cracked a joke saying,
"Oh Judy, get over it." When I didn't get it he said, "Oh
Judy, you're still slow." This was his way of being funny;
he would reference people as a different gender—very
gay humor. Because of the closeness Steve and I had
this made me smile and become more alert. We were
just like family.

Steve also thanked me for being there for him when
he was living. He explained he wasn't very good at
communicating or showing appreciation, which was
very true of him. He wasn't a person who showed
warm emotion. I would know he liked someone
when he teased him or her a lot—as he did me. This
communication with him was a validation to me of
our close friendship and it brought me warm-hearted
feelings about the times we shared. In the moment
I felt it was as important to him as it was to me to
reconnect.

These moments were very loving and insightful, most
of them being very personal and hard to write about.
I know I have freewill; I do not live my life directly
by what I am told. Instead I use this information to
enhance my life.

The reading was very therapeutic for me, but it also seemed really surreal. I was in a room talking to spirit who was giving me a wealth of accurate information and I fought to suspend judgment. I continually asked, "Is this real?"

Even grandmothers can come through with the bits of information that would not mean anything to a by-stander but the whole world to the sitter, such as Jerry's grandmother stating his partner is a "chip-a-holic." For me and even the reader this is silly information to know, but because it was confronted Jerry and his partner are now more aware of what they are feeding themselves. This little habit was the foundation of a better diet thanks to Grandmother.

Personally, my biggest surprise guest was...well let me explain it like you were there from the beginning. I was giving a phone session and as usual the spirit came early to meditate with me about the sitter. When I began to look over the spirit he seemed somewhat familiar. He was wearing a cowboy outfit, neatly pressed, 1950's Hollywood style, not like the real cowboys. It dawned on me that it was John Wayne and I got extremely excited. This is my first famous dead person! Yes, I got giddy, until I was corrected and told he was not John Wayne.

"Oh. Sorry to assume." Then I became flat out embarrassed and let it go. When the sitter called from California I began to tell him who was here in spirit and what they were wearing. I also shared my funny mistaken identity story. The sitter then told me he knew who it was. It was Roc Hudson. Roc Hudson!

Roc Hudson is in my house talking to me, how strange! The reading went extremely well. He is a kind, gentle man and very well spoken. In fact he kept mentioning his voice quality to me and how he worked very hard on it. So I complemented him on his deep voice. Before he left I asked him if he could send over Elvis for me. Elvis is one of my biggest crushes of all times. I had a framed picture of him in my room when I was a little girl. I would have loved to have met him. Roc smiled real polite and said, "What do you need to talk to him for? Take care. Good bye."

Mr. Hudson did not act in many cowboy style movies but I got on the internet and found the movie in which he wore the same cowboy outfit he wore to my house. I also discovered he had surgery to deepen his voice.

Well it does get strange around here, and surprises pop up all the time. When I do get the chance to meet Elvis I will be sure to let you know how he is.

I have learned to repeat everything I hear even if it is really awkward. My favorite was when a spirit started singing "We're off to see the Wizard..." I looked at the sitter and said, "I am sorry I don't have a singing voice but....." and begun to recite what the guide was saying. This guide was by far the most flamboyant spirit I have come to meet. He showed up in my office with Mark, the sitter, wearing a pink feather boa, bright blue pants and a glitter dipped t-shirt. This was a huge contrast to the sitter who dressed in business wear. At first I wondered if I had the right guides, but within the first two words I said about the male spirit in the room, Mark knew exactly who it was. It was James.

We're Off to See the Wizard
Mark, 36, corporate trainer, Atlanta, GA

I was cautious when I arrived at Jamie's home. However, once we sat down and began to talk I became very much at ease. Jamie didn't ask any leading questions. As a matter of fact she did most of the talking, giving me details about her dog and so forth—making small talk. Then while we were talking she mentioned specifically two guides had arrived, one female and one male. The female identified was my grandmother. Before Jamie could describe the male, I knew it was James. He kept interrupting my grandmother. When he was living he was always anxious to speak and typically he wanted to be the center of attention.

Once our focus turned to James it was as though I was reunited with an old friend. The first thing James said was, "I really want to thank you for everything you did. You held through and you didn't leave me. Thank you."

When James became ill he had no one to turn to. His family was not a healthy option and I was all he had. The situation was so hard at times that I was not sure I could continue. Near the end I spoke to his family, but they were not very accepting of the idea of having to care for him. So James remained with me until he passed away from complications of AIDS, which was four years ago.

During the reading, in standard James fashion, he had to lighten things up. "Didn't I pass gracefully?" he inquired. James' passing was not graceful and it was like him to make a grand joke of it. The morning of his passing no one from his family was available when the moment came to put him on life support. This left the nurses no choice but to go through with the procedure. It was James' last struggle and he fought it hard. I was there and witnessed his death. It was the last time I saw him alive and when Jamie referred to this I knew exactly what James' was talking about.

From the beginning of our friendship, James loved my dog Bo. During the latter stages of his illness when he was bed-ridden, Bo became even more important to him. She would not leave his side. Through Jamie he asked, "When is she going to get a hair cut? You need to watch how much she is eating, Daddy. That food you have—it's good but try the senior brand. Less calories."

James would refer to me as Daddy when talking about Bo. She is fifteen years old and a relative takes care of her now because I travel frequently. I called to find out if what was said during the reading was accurate. I was told her hair has not been cut and is so long it drags the floor. I also learned she has in fact gained some weight. Then he sang the words from the *Wizard of Oz*. "We're off to see the Wizard. Roar!" He used to pick Bo up and run with her imitating the wicked witch saying, "I've got you now, my little pretty." It was so amazing to hear these memories brought up by him again.

I clearly saw James' personality and mannerisms when he mentioned an individual I am interested in romantically. When I asked how long should I wait to see if this situation would work, he replied, "Honey, this is a good catch so let's not push it." That was a classic James statement. He amended his advice by telling me to keep my friend around because he thinks his workout partner is cute. As Jamie relayed James' description of this person she put her fingertips to the center of her chest and ran them straight across from shoulder to shoulder. This was how James would refer to his "tall glass of water," in other words a guy he found attractive.

Lastly, Jamie asked me what was significant about the month of October -narrowing. Then she narrowed it to the 16th of October. The 16th was the last day James was able to speak to me. He passed the following day. There is no way Jamie could have known these dates and their significance. Most of these memories were buried deep in my mind and I had not thought about the details since James passed.

My experience with Jamie was extremely settling for me. It has helped me grow personally and given me confidence in my own spirituality. It has definitely brought me closer to God.

After the session Mark explained how James loved to dress up and roller skate through the house with his dog Bo. It is good to see we retain who we love to be – unique personalities.

Another aspect of readings I enjoy is to see people come closer to their inner peace. Mark mentions how his reading "brought me [him] closer to God." Even though there was no conversation about religion, spirituality, or belief. The simple reconnection of family and friends who have passed gave the sitter feelings of inner peace, hope or faith.

Reconnecting with an old family member or friend unexpectedly can bring up many deep emotions. I have no doubt in my mind spirit wait until the perfect time to present themselves, whether the sitter is prepared or not. A few years ago, I was at my step mom's family reunion in upstate New York for the fourth of July when I was presented an opportunity to reunite two old friends. I was sitting by myself at a table outside, next to one of the Finger Lakes, finishing my dinner when a group of distant cousins I had met earlier that evening came to sit with me.

Off the cuff one of the cousins mentioned I gave a reading

to their mother and would I, could I give a short reading to them right now? Before I replied a spirit named Beth appeared next to us at the table. She was in her late twenties, wearing a summery yellow outfit with matching sandals to boot and had a great sense of humor and peace about her. She wanted to talk to her friend. "Would you please tell her that I am okay? I can explain everything."

I acknowledged Beth but told everyone at the table I would go around and give short direct messages to each one, leaving Beth to be the last to talk. I had a feeling this was important and I wanted to be sure her friend at the table had the option of talking privately with me in case this was too personal for the others to hear.

When it was Beth's turn I described her appearance and age to her friend.

"Yellow is Beth's favorite color! And that is like her to wear the matching sandals. It's her. That's Beth." Her friend confessed to the table that the descriptions match up.

I followed Beth's lead and began to translate her experience of being caught in the Twin Towers. I was timid about sharing this in front of the others but the young woman at the table gave permission to continue.

"I know it is not like me to not call," she explained, "but I couldn't reach my purse. You see I had a meeting in another room when the plane hit. I thought maybe it was a bomb or something. Then there was a rumor that it was a plane, but it sounded so unbelievable."

Her friend began to tear up and talk aloud to Beth, agreeing with what she was saying.

Based on how Beth carried herself I knew she was the type of person who maintains composure, and she immediately wanted to clarify what steps she had taken. "Anyways, all the telephones were knocked out of service because the plane hit below the floor we were on. I was in the glass meeting room with the door closed so the smoke did not come in right away; we could see it build up in the offices outside. I think we were in shock because none of us reacted right away. I decided I was going for my purse to get my phone, but the fumes, the heat and the smell of gas were overwhelming. I never really felt panicked, or frantic. I saw the others try to make it to the stairwells and windows for air but I started to get really dizzy and nauseous like I was going to faint from the smoke inhalation."

The friend exclaimed to the others present, "I knew it, isn't that what I told you happened to Beth!?"

Beth didn't miss a beat, "It was weird and comforting; I got this complete sense of peace. I thought I was going to sleep. I don't remember trying to escape or falling to the floor. I don't even remember the building collapsing, or needing air. I never got to my phone. Don't feel sorry for me. I am doing all right…I really wanted to tell you that I love you and thank you for talking with my family, especially my dad…" Beth went on giving personal messages for her family. She wanted desperately for her family to stop imaging a horrible death for her. Beth made it clear; her passing was a peaceful one even amidst a terrifying atmosphere.

When Beth bid her farewell, we all sat at the table stunned, unprepared for what Beth had actually shared with us. What an amazing encounter. I felt very privileged to have been the translator for Beth. Her story helped us all become aware to the different experience people had with in the Towers. Through Beth we were able to talk about 9.11 and heal our wounds a little more.

Chapter
— ELEVEN —

International Relations

*"One does not discover new lands without consenting
to lose sight of the shore for a very long time."*
—Andre Gide

No two cultures approach spirituality in the exact same way. Growing up in the United States with Western Philosophies influencing how one perceives life, one tends to become more scientific. As a people we demand more proof behind the unexplainable since our culture generally keeps the intuitive, psychic knowledge as a novelty. Even though we are on the verge of breaking through, we still have a ways to go.

Although I consider myself to be very spiritual I do not perform any rituals or special routines and have no demands for a specific environment when I work. In Brazil many said my work is very 'scientific,' which humors me because in the United States skeptics remind me my work is not scientifically based. In fact my work is often considered frou-frou. The surprising outcome from this inconsistency between cultural expectations is the information that comes through during readings is exact, regardless of the country I am in, no matter how I conduct my sessions. Beyond the language barrier and cultural differences, the connection to spirit blankets us all and has no prejudices. We are all under one sky.

My first trip to Brazil was anything but normal. Rui, my best friend, did not know the extent of my abilities as a clairvoyant. I kept this side of me private from him. Rui never asked so I didn't tell, until we visited his mother Ana in Brazil.

When his family and friends decided to have an Umbanda session they were quite worried I would not understand what was going on or at the least I might be frightened by it; not to mention the session was spoken in Portuguese, which I do not speak nor understand. The family hosting the sessions is very close with Ana and their history together runs long; they are considered family. The "family" agreed I should not attend. All Rui had to do was approach me with the idea of the session and I was begging to be there. I explained off the top what I could do and how the sessions would probably be similar to the channeling sessions I had attended in Mount Dora, FL. with Ola. (Ola is a spirit who channels to groups of people teaching about the enlightening growth of life. She suggests her attendees wear white and clean their auras before her session begins.)

Once Rui informed his family they agreed I could sit in. I was told to wear all white and follow Rui's lead if I was asked to do anything by spirit. That night we gathered on the downstairs concrete porch located in the rear of the house. It was painted white with tropical plants lining the perimeter and a picnic table off to the side. The only clear altar was the one located on several built in shelves centered on the east wall. On the altar were shells, incense, plant leaves, candles and several small wooden and ceramic figures representing the Gods, Goddess, and spirit beings who protect them. The figurines were arranged based upon their level of enlightenment. The slaves were on the bottom shelf, then working their way up through saints, Gods, and Goddesses to the angels positioned at the top self.

I was given a place to sit, paper and coloured pencils

so I could draw what I saw and translate any messages I received. After I completed my intent I looked up to a porch full of spirit, but there was something strange about where they were. They were not bunched together, which is how I am used to seeing them, they appeared to be assigned or protecting specific areas of the room. I began to sketch each one and where I saw them while the session began. Umbanda, to my surprise, has many similarities to Native American rituals. Sage and the use of directions: North, South, East and West, to cleanse a room and auras were all related. I was thrilled. I began to question the spirit beings who had arrived for more commonalities and dictated them to my paper.

After the four hour session was complete I went inside to compare notes with Monica, Rui's unrelated sister, and asked to speak with Terezinha, the woman who channeled the whole time. The locations of spirit were explained first. Within the area of the porch there are actually several altars. Each spirit has a specific place to present them. I had accurately drawn and located each spirit's description and placement. We were off to a good start. I went on reading my notes about the rituals and why they were used but the specific messages for the individuals I was not privy to. All of what I understood during the four hour Portuguese sessions was precisely what had occurred.

The kicker is, several months before my arrival, Monica's mother Fernanda had been asking for a seer to come and sit in her sessions to give added proof that what she was doing was real. There was never any doubt on her behalf, but she needed the answers to know if she should continue hosting the Umbanda sessions at her home. After I was told about this, Fernanda and I had a good laugh and talked in length about coincidence. This was the beginning of my relationship with Monica and her family.

From Brazil to Portugal

My name is Monica, I am thirty years old and I was born in Luanda, Angola. I currently live in Recife, Brazil, the place I refer to as home.

My family introduced me to spirituality at an early age. My parents' openness to this idea and Brazil's general acceptance of spirituality makes the whole concept natural to me. In Brazil spirituality falls under various traditions: Umbanda, Candomble, Cardecism, amongst others. I was mostly exposed to Umbanda, which follows an African ritualistic approach to spirituality and also pays respect to the saints and religious dates of Catholicism.

During an Umbanda session everyone dresses in white. The individuals who channel, known as mediums, are at different levels of spiritual development. Their level determines their ability and to whom they can communicate. The mediums can channel with spirits of higher and lower light, and they may vary from native Indians, African slaves and lost souls to saints of the Catholic religion.

In contrast to all my previous experiences of spirituality, Jamie showed me a new way of working with spirits. Jamie's method is not tied to religious ceremony, but equally seems to aim to deliver personal inner peace and well being. I find Jamie exceptionally gifted because not only can she channel, she can read auras and consciously see and talk to spirits too.

From the various consultations with Jamie, I was delighted to discover new and different ways of working spiritually. In the process of learning from Jamie's guides, I was amazed and surprised to have Jamie put me in touch with my personal guides. A lot of people I know would have been skeptical to this type of advice, but questioning the legitimacy of Jamie's channeling was not an issue for me. The guidance my family received from Jamie was too specific to be something made up.

The following are just a few examples of Jamie's channeling for my family.

Are You Sure He is There?

Jamie first channeled for my family at our home in Recife. Little Maitland came through first. After briefly introducing herself, she went straight into talking about our family's tire business. Maitland told us she entered our tire store – Jamie had never been there – and described each of our fifteen employees. She told us where each person sits, gave physical traits, and explained their job responsibilities. Maitland even commented on what we think of each of them. I was absolutely thrilled about how correct this all was. We had only recently become the owners of the business and it was comforting to gain reassurance we were on the right track.

While Maitland described the store and employees, she also depicted the office layout. My mom had made a couple of billboards with red cloth that needed to be hung on the walls. The idea was to use the billboards for information, pictures and interesting articles for our employees. My mom and I had mentioned on several occasions that it was high time to actually put them up.

As Maitland entered my mom's office she said, "Aren't those red billboards lying in the corner supposed to be hung on the walls?" Guess what we did the next day at work?

Maitland then told us about some of the spirits that accompany each of my family members. Maitland described my grandfather, who had passed away when I was nine years old, to my dad. I can still recall how my dad held back the tears in the corner of his eyes. My family was separated from their relatives in 1975, when civil war broke out in Angola. We moved to Brazil while most of our relatives, including my dad's father, moved to Portugal. This caused my dad to have the opportunity to see his father only twice in the eight years between their separation and Grandfather's death.

My father looked at Maitland with an expression that said, "Are you sure he is there?" Maitland sensed his doubt and asked him to come closer to her. She then said, "Your father asked me to do this." She gently reached for his head with her right hand, keeping her fingers close together, and touched him softly three times on the head, just like my grandfather used to do to him when he was a kid. That was the proof he needed. Maitland's optimism, kindness, and the way she delivers positive and negative news, makes me feel secure and contemplative. It was a privilege to encounter Maitland and I am grateful for all her help and encouragement.

After this session with Maitland, Jamie followed up with a private reading for my dad. This was extremely important for him because he was beginning to work spiritually, learning how to communicate with his guides, and allowing them to use his body for channeling.

Jamie was able to describe the spirits who were close to him and with whom he was beginning to work. My mom and I were familiar with these spirits because my dad had began receiving them on a regular basis. Jamie; however, had never seen my dad work so we knew she didn't base her descriptions on her own experience. She drew each of these guides and discussed their appearance. We know what they look like because when spirits channel through they tell us what they look like even though we cannot see them.

We never doubted the guides we worked with previously, but we welcomed this extra confirmation of their existence. My dad was particularly reassured and felt encouraged to go on with his mission of helping others through channeling.

Only Eight Days After

After I met Jamie in Brazil, I told my friends in Portugal all about her. They had spiritual experiences during their holidays in Brazil, now they were curious and excited to meet Jamie. A few months after my first meeting with Jamie, I organized a visit to Portugal. A couple of days before I arrived in Lisbon, my Portuguese great-aunt, Alaide, passed away from cancer. This became the main subject of my session with Jamie.

Jamie channeled a spirit called Grace, an English lady. Grace described Alaide in detail. Speaking via Grace, Alaide said she was glad to have her hair back and happy to be with us again. I was communicating with

Alaide only eight days after she passed away.

Alaide asked me to do a few things for her. She requested me to tell her husband to open the big windows of the house every morning. The maid was to clean her favorite pieces of china and silver, and continue buying her husband's favorite bread and cheese every morning. Alaide also sent a message for her two daughters to get an envelope she had left for them next to her bed and to act upon it only after her husband passes.

I was pleased to hear from my great aunt, but I was slightly worried about how to share this information with her daughters. I decided to approach Ana Bela, the oldest daughter, since she knows about my family's spiritual practices.

As soon as we sat down in the café Ana Bela asked me if I had a message to give her about her mom. I looked at her with amazement as a chill went through my body. She knew exactly why we were meeting because she had an intuition about it. After delivering Alaide's messages, Ana Bela explained their meanings.

Since Alaide passed away, her husband had wanted things to remain exactly the way they were when my aunt was alive. This is why he hadn't been opening the windows. But Alaide, who had loved the fresh breeze, felt the house needed some fresh air, and this explained why she asked for the windows to be opened daily. Ana Bela pointed out that her mother was always keen to have the house looking its best, as if she would receive guests at any minute. Everything was always proper and orderly. It was like one of those houses in the movies. However, Ana Bela's father no longer allowed the maid to clean the room where all the china and silver were. He wanted to make sure one of Alaide's favorite places in the house remained the same, but she wanted everything cleaned the way it had always been.

When Alaide was living, her maid used to buy her husband's favorite bread and cheese each day. Towards the end of her days, when Alaide's cancer worsened, the maid stopped buying her husband's bread and cheese. Even after her passing, Alaide continues looking after her husband. The envelope that I told Ana Bela about turned out to be a letter and a testament to the daughters. It was next to the bed, as described by Alaide, and had still not been opened.

After talking with Ana Bela, I could feel her happiness to know her mom was doing well. Alaide's detailed channeled messages via Grace now made sense. I also felt great comfort in hearing from Alaide, and knowing that somehow, somewhere, she is doing fine.

Apartment for Sale

My dad has a few apartments in Portugal. Needing money, he decided to put one on the market. Selling the apartment was turning out to be a difficult task; it normally takes a very long time to sell in the Portuguese real estate market.

I called Jamie hoping to get advice from any of the guides. She helped me long distance. She contacted her guides and they said in a maximum time of four months the apartment would be sold for a very specific amount.

My dad contacted his lawyer in Lisbon to explain the advice given via Jamie. The lawyer could not believe it because he knew the difficult local market conditions. He was only open to the idea of it because he had the experience of spiritual sessions both in Brazil and with Jamie. A couple weeks later the attorney called my father with an offer. The price was less than what Jamie's guides had mentioned. My dad decided to take the offer since he was keen in selling the apartment. The day the lawyer was to close the sale the buyers failed to show up and the whole deal — cancelled.

Two months later my father received a call from his attorney informing him of another offer he received. This bid was for the amount detailed in the spiritual session with Jamie. Within the four-month time frame foretold by spirits, the apartment was sold, the papers were signed and everything was settled.

Our meeting has been such a blessing for us both. Monica and I still teach each other about our ways of spirituality. During our visits I have noticed how spirit seem to merge extreme international opposite beliefs to fit under one umbrella, by giving us the explanation of where the belief came from. Our interactions allow everyone involved to grow. I hope in the future I will be able to share these findings publicly. Until then I look forward to spending time in other nations exploring their unique beliefs.

This following story came in an unusual way. My friend, Brian, arranged an opportunity of a lifetime for me to meet Robert Swan, the first person to walk to both the North and South poles entirely unaided.

"This is Jamie. She is a massage therapist...and a psychic."

I always wince when people say this—it just sounds weird. Robert turned his blue-washed stare on me and said, "You should meet my friend Emma." He then told us about a twist in his polar quest that he never mentions publicly— "for obvious reasons," he said.

When Robert had, after seven years of pleading for funds, finally got ready to leave from a London dock bound for New Zealand and Antarctica, he suffered a crushing blow. The insurance company decided his ship needed additional fittings costing $150,000 or they would not be allowed to leave—and it had to be done in two weeks. The Pack Ice, which surrounds Antarctica, is only open to ships for two months a year and, if you miss this weather window, you have to wait a whole year to try again. Robert did not have the funds to sustain the project for another year, and to not leave would spell a total collapse of the expedition as well as personal bankruptcy for Robert.

After one week things looked grim, with all sponsorship sources fully tapped, there was still $100,000 to find. That very morning an old lady boarded the expedition ship 'Southern Quest' and quietly informed Robert that a man, short in stature, with short grey hair and glasses that lived far away across the sea was going to support him. Robert dismissed this as a fantasy and thought no more of it until three days later a check for $100,000 arrived from Sir Jack Hayward, who lived in the Bahamas. This man was 5'7", had short grey hair and wore glasses; Robert had never met Sir Jack in his life.

The expedition was on and so was the hunt to find the mysterious old lady. Emma was found: she had no knowledge of Sir Jack, but said she saw a "picture" of him in her mind while listening to Robert pleading for contributions on Public Radio. Robert instructed his crew that Emma could spend as much time as she wished on board

"Southern Quest"—he thought her a good luck charm. Only days before leaving, Emma was found deep in the engine room taking out two shopping bags that seemed a little heavy for her. And upon departure Emma told Robert he and his companions would not die on their Polar journey, "You'll be alright, dear."

Robert now looked at me and I sensed his implied question.

"Yes, she must be your Earth Angel," I said quietly.

Again he gave me his wintry stare, as if weighing whether to go further...and continued his story. On Jan 11th, 1986, when Robert and his team arrived exhausted at the South Pole—after 70 days and 900 miles on foot—, they were greeted with the news that 'Southern Quest' had been crushed and sunk by freak ice in Antarctic waters. There were no fatalities but Robert wondered what Emma might have to say on the matter.

Months later, after a desperate battle against the elements, the media, and finances, Robert went to see Emma in her tiny East London flat. She greeted him as if he were expected and congratulated him on the team's achievement on reaching the South Pole. Then, very matter-of-factly, she handed him the two shopping bags, which she had removed from 'Southern Quest' 15 months previously. Robert stood holding the bags, completely nonplussed.

Emma smiled and said, "I knew you would reach the South Pole, Robert, but I also knew that 'Southern Quest' would be lost to the power of the pack ice. In these bags are some scraps of metal I found at the bottom of the engine room and I thought then that you might like to have them as a memento."

Robert looked at us. "That's Emma." She has been a part of his life ever since and is now over 90 years old.

As Robert and Brian talked on, I suddenly got a familiar buzz in my ears; I broke into a sweat; and I felt certain my ears were glowing red. I told Robert there was someone present who wanted to talk to him –it was his Grandfather on his father's side and he was very vocal and insistent. "Right", said Robert, "I know who you mean. He was a real hard case." I told him some of the things his Grandfather was saying, but we agreed Robert should have a proper reading. This is his account.

To The Artic and Beyond
Robert Swan, 47, Explorer, England

I was immediately impressed with Jamie's no-nonsense approach to the reading: no mumbo-jumbo, just in and on. My Grandfather was there at once and he made it clear he knew everybody in our family thought him a complete "asshole"; he advised me not to walk over people as he had; he apologized for having always pushed in his life; and he strongly advised me not to just do, but to relax and live a little. He went on to warning me I was in danger of going down the same track and if I just kept pushing and doing, I would be remembered as a real asshole too.

I would say that my Grandfather was a real hard man, who had risen from being a laborer in a highway crew and through his own determination and focus, had amassed considerable wealth. He had often behaved in an appalling way to our family. I do not wish to share his ways and means, but tough is an understatement. Divide to rule was his clear tool of power. In the reading he made it very clear that he had been a deeply unhappy man and was now full of serious remorse for how he behaved. His warning for me not to travel the same road was serious: but, more importantly, the clarity and timing of his warning showed me that I had begun a drift into unhappiness without admitting it to myself. I am thankful to him for the stern admonition.

Next to emerge was his wife, my Grandmother. She appeared to be in a very jolly and happy state, which was in sharp contrast to my memories of her as being quite oppressed and low spirited – indeed my Grandfather had created a feeling of unhappiness around him. I realize now that was the point: because my Grandmother said, in her reading, that her marriage was truly "until death do us part." They were both there together for me in the reading, but otherwise very much apart. Death, for her, had been liberation from his oppression.

Grandmother also had a blunt warning for me on my health: she said, "Keep up your physical health; it is what keeps you here on Earth." Within a week of the reading I became a non-smoker, after 20 years. Only a smoker would know what this entails.

I also recall that on my first meeting with Jamie, before any readings, she had observed an old injury lying deep in my shoulder which was causing some imbalance – I had been astonished by her observance. It seems that my years of living in danger, and the risk to life and limb, were finally taking their toll on me. I was no longer invincible. At age 47, I was perhaps still in time to heed the advice of my Grandmother.

After this timely blast from the Grandparents I met a mystery man, called Richard, who would not give his second name. He was an explorer/scientist from the late 1800's who had been a real forerunner on the environment, and had died on a journey near a cold ocean. He was very positive that my efforts on the environment were worthwhile and he challenged me to find his name.

Attempting to inspire people into doing more for the environment is now my passion and my life. This quest has caused me to present our achievements before the World Earth Summits at Rio de Janeiro in 1992 and in Johannesburg in 2002. However, this effort often falls rather flat in a world that is "consumed by consuming"...and it often feels like a total uphill battle; yet, here was this voice from the past urging me on, telling me that it was worth it − perhaps even the inspirers need inspiration. Don't' worry Richard, I will find you − your challenge has been laid down, and I will not forget to meet it.

I was impressed with Robert's reading, indeed, as I am with the others. But what was interesting in this case was that a man, who owed his very survival to scientific calculation, would be so open to the spiritual side of life. The slightest navigational error on a great white ice sheet the size of the USA would result in death.

Robert explained to me, "We had to make decisions that confronted our sanity: survival is not just a physical being; it is also a fight to remain sane, a fight not to go mad." He figured out that in order to trap his mind, he would become it, and go back into it. He looked at me and said "I became my life, to stay alive, to stay sane." Robert favored me with a moody smile. "My introspection kept me alive. Why would this be unusual?"

Once more I was subjected to that intense blue stare that is so arresting. I later learned his eyes had changed to the pale blue colour and the skin on his face blistered off, as a result of the hole in the ozone layer over the South Pole.

To know more about Robert Swan's mission in life to clean up the world go to www.missionantarctica.com to read a compelling interview with him or head to his website http://www.2041.com/ to learn more about his programs, lectures and trips to the Antarctica.

In completing this book, I realized how true the statement that helped start this whole affair is; psychic phenomena can only be confirmed one person at a time as each individual encounters their own validating experience. I am thankful to the many people who wanted to share their experiences with *With Love and Light*. You have been a great inspiration to me and have been a daily reminder of how one person can make a difference.

There are no coincidences in life. This book has attracted itself to you for one reason or another. If through this experience, you have a chance to reconnect to spirit through the many channels available, seize it. As I have said before and now have had my chance to show you, unlock your doors, it is safe.

Acknowledgements

I would like to take the time to give my thanks and gratitude to the following people and places. By no means could there be any order to the below list, for every person mentioned should be placed at the top. A special thank you to my Dad, **Joel**, for suggesting I write *With Love and Light*. Dad, thank you for listening to all my wild stories, and never once loosing faith in my ability. You are an amazing soul. When I grow up, I want to be just like you. To **Rui**, my forever man, for not reading a single word of your wife's "baby" until the book was published. You remained a constant unbiased grounding force, which I needed to keep in the moment and out of my computer. I love you. **Luca and Malu** who joined me after this trip was done. Thank you for adding a bigger dose of humility to me and creating feelings inside of me I had no idea you could have on Earth. **Joyce Ann,** thank you for the gift of life and creativity. You always showed me there were no boundaries and taught me, by example, the many qualities of love. **Jane**, thank you for your guidance and most of all your curiosity. You have sparked a definite desire within me to share and teach others. To **Dale,** for never worrying about me and showing how unconditional love spans through extended family. **ML** and **Granddaddy Jones,** you both are very close to my heart. Thank you LeaRoy for coming to see me and showing me that death is just another step in life. I love you the mostest. A big thank you to **Jason** for fixing my computer and making life easier for me. I love you brother. You are my mentor. **Edie,** for being the next in line and hopefully followed by **Liv. Lucy,** thank you for listening to my ideas and always asking how the book is. Your curiosity is contagious! To **Vanessa,** for encouragement and your ability to be super anal. This book would not be as clean as it is without you. **Nana** and **Carol** for convincing me this gift is not as scary as I thought it would be, but more importantly encouraging me to continue on. Thank you to the **unseen world. Elise Anderson** for lunches and the best smile. **Marguerite** for being an understanding teacher with a sneaky side. See... your students do go on to do great things. I love you endlessly for everything you have done for me. **Penny D.** for table talk advice. A huge thank you to **Robert Swan** for being so incredible, kind, and cutting edge. You can save the world. **Maddie dog** for her separation anxiety, whines, loyalty and love. Hot legs mail man. I don't think I need to say more here. Thank you to **every client** who had willingness to send in a story, they all played a big part in this book. Thank you to all my clients for their trust in my abilities. Poopette, **Frank's** endearing word. You are a muse to me. **Mary Martin** for sitting with me while I write this book, again and again. I miss the friendship you gave. A very special thank you to dear **Tina Rock** for putting this book together. For a new editor you really have it going on. *With Love and Light* would have no shape without you! **CBFA.** You gave me the "matrix graph", "KHITB", "golden nugget", "show don't tell", "widows and orphans", "it's your turn to sit in the chair" and most importantly to me you gave your love, dedication, and are the model of whom I wish to mimic myself after. You are selfless yet strong and have taught me how to express my feelings in words. You have challenged me to fullest without stepping on my toes. May the Gods look down favorably upon you. See you on the flip side.